What Does
the Bible
Say About... **?**

Angels
and Demons

"What Does the Bible Say About...?" Series
Ronald D. Witherup, P.S.S.
Series Editor

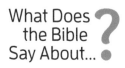

What Does the Bible Say About...?

Angels and Demons

John Gillman and Clifford M. Yeary

New City Press
Hyde Park, New York

Published by New City Press
202 Comforter Blvd.,
Hyde Park, NY 12538
www.newcitypress.com

Cover design and layout by Miguel Tejerina

Biblical citations are taken from the New Revised Standard Version
©1989 Division of Christian Education of the National Council of the
Churches of Christ in the United States of America.

Library of Congress Cataloging-in-Publication Data
What does the Bible say about Angels and Demons
Library of Congress Control Number: 2020952646

ISBN: 978-1-56548-379-8
ISBN: 978-1-56548-380-4 (e-book)
ISBN: 978-1-56548-697-3 (series ISBN)

2nd Printing, December 2022

Printed in the United States of America

Contents

Series Preface

The Bible remains the world's number one best-seller of all time. Millions of copies in more than two thousand languages and dialects are sold every year, yet how many are opened and read on a regular basis? Despite the impression the Bible's popularity might give, its riches are not easy to mine. Its message is not self-evident and is sometimes hard to relate to our daily lives.

This series addresses the need for a reliable guide to reading the Bible profitably. Each volume is designed to unlock the Bible's mysteries for the interested reader who asks, "What does the Bible say about...?" Each book addresses a timely theme in contemporary culture, based upon questions people are asking today, and explaining how the Bible can speak to these questions as reflected in both Old and New Testaments.

Ideal for individual or group study, each volume consists of short, concise chapters on a biblical theme in non-technical language, and in a style accessible to all. The expert authors have been chosen for their knowledge of the Bible. While taking into account current scholarship, they know how to explain the Bible's teaching in simple language. They are also able to relate the biblical message to the challenges of today's Church and society while avoiding a simplistic use of the biblical text for trying to "prove" a point or defend a position, which is called "prooftexting"—an improper use of the Bible. The focus in these books is on a religious perspective, explaining what the Bible says, or does not say, about each theme. Short discussion questions invite sharing and reflection.

So, take up your Bible with confidence, and with your guide explore "what the Bible says about ANGELS AND DEMONS."

Introduction*

Angels and demons and dragons, oh my! Our world is populated by many natural wonders, but faith and imagination have always countenanced the existence of beings of great wonder beyond the reach of our five senses. In the last few decades, while adherence to religion has been in decline, angels have made a comeback. One author has observed that "the angel and demon binary still inhabits huge swathes of cultural space in the technophilic twenty-first century,"[1] and another that "books on angels are as numerous as the celestial choirs themselves."[2] They appear in TV series, films, and art. We hear of them in stories and read about them in autobiographies and novels.[3]

Perhaps you too have had your own experience with these heavenly beings. However, not only angels, but demons too populate contemporary imagination, and, more ominously—according to many—are at work in the world creating havoc, causing destruction, and enticing fallible humans away from noble aspirations.

The biblical world of both the Old and New Testaments mapped a universe smaller than the one we

---

* In this co-authored work, Clifford Yeary wrote an initial draft of the introduction and the first five chapters and then had to withdraw from the project. John Gillman edited and amplified these chapters significantly and authored chapters six and seven and the afterword.

now know as nearly infinite. To the biblical writers, the world encompassed three heavens: one of the sky overhead, filled with sun and moon and stars; a second "firmament" that held the waters that fell through the sky as rain and snow; and above that a third heaven, where God and his angels held court and ruled over the earth below. Angels appear throughout the Bible from Genesis to Revelation, and demons from Leviticus to Revelation; the serpent—though not yet identified as a demon—first shows up in Genesis.

The English word *angel* derives from the Latin *angelus*, which refers to a messenger from the heavenly sphere to the earthly sphere. In the Hebrew Bible and its Greek translation, the Septuagint, the terms for messenger are, respectively, *malak* and *angelos*. These terms are used for both heavenly *and* earthly messengers, a range of meaning broader than the English *angel*. Thus, a human person may also serve as a messenger to another—sharing a blessing, offering encouragement, or bringing comfort. In those instances, such a messenger may truly seem like an angel. In addition, sometimes a heavenly messenger in the Bible may at first appear as a human before being recognized as an angel. While there is a linguistic overlap in the biblical use of the term "messenger," there remains a clear practical distinction between earthly and celestial messengers.

Today, astrophysicists contemplate many mysterious energies present and at work in our universe, but they rarely, if ever, allow for the possibility of angels and demons, let alone dragons. And yet our culture remains fascinated with them. Many believe in the reality of angels and fear demons. An Associated Press poll in 2011 found that nearly eight in ten Americans (77 percent) believe angels exist.[4] The same poll showed that 94 percent of those who attend religious services, 88 percent of Christians, and over 40 percent of people who never attend religious services believe that angels exist.

As a culture, many of us enjoy contemplating the possibility that we are part of a divine plan, but we are not always sure how that plan works or where we fit into it. People whose beliefs are open to the existence of spiritual beings, angelic or otherwise, may look to connect with a dimension of reality that transcends the confines of their material existence.

While angels testify to the presence of the Divine, demons and dragons often, though not always, represent a more sinister side of cosmic forces. Demons refer to evil spirits and dragons to a legendary serpentine or reptilian creature. Dragons have soared back into popularity in recent years, in children's animated movies, like *How to Train Your Dragon* (and its two sequels), in blockbuster 3D films like *Avatar*, and in the adult-themed HBO series *Game of Thrones*. Recall that English literature began with a tale of dragons and their mortal enemies in *Beowulf* (written as early as 700 AD); in many modern tales, by contrast, dragons and people have become more than friends—many stories describe a powerful, lifelong psychic link bonding human riders to these powerful flying beasts. Dragons may symbolize many intuitive responses to what remains strange and powerful in a world and cosmos beyond our limited comprehension. Little wonder, then, that dragons are presented to us as beasts to be greatly feared or cautiously befriended. In the Bible, dragons may be related to the beast known as Leviathan, the multi-headed sea serpent in Psalm 74:14, or to the seven-headed dragon, the most sinister of creatures, in the Book of Revelation (12:3). Both symbolize ultimate evil and are a direct challenge to the authority of God.

Angels and demons are, if not dominant in, then surely part of the fabric of contemporary culture. They appear from time to time in biblical passages and are defined in the *Catechism of the Catholic Church*.[5] It is important to recall that Catholic teaching about them is subordinate to the more central and important truths of faith. Belief in angels, although evident in the biblical world and the broader Near Eastern cultural environment of the time, is only alluded to as an article of faith in the Nicene Creed ("I believe in one God, / . . . maker of heaven and earth, / of all things visible and invisible"), for example. These heavenly beings are venerated but not worshipped in the liturgical tradition.

All three Abrahamic religions—Judaism, Christianity, and Islam—have traditions about angels and demons that have not given rise to major dogmatic differences. These religions display more common ground than distinctive teaching about such spiritual beings that interact with humans, often in surprising ways. The influence of the Hebrew Bible and the deuterocanonical books of the Old

Testament, wherein angels are commonplace, on the latter two faiths is evident. This will be particularly apparent as we explore how the presence of angels and demons in the Old Testament carries over into the New Testament, and from there into our cultural context.

As we explore in the pages ahead how angels, demons, and dragons are traditionally represented in biblical literature, we will also discuss how they are depicted in much of our entertainment media. In doing that, we will also consider how the Bible might yet have something of real significance to say about angels and demons. Oh my!

Chapter One

When Angels Come Visiting

Shakespeare was well aware of ethereal beings that transcend our senses. Hamlet, on seeing the ghost of his father, petitions that "Angels and ministers of grace defend us!" (Act 1, Scene 4). This theme of defending and ministering angels is reminiscent of their role during and after the temptation of Jesus by the devil (Matthew 4:1–11). One scene later in the Bard's play, Hamlet assures a skeptical Horatio that, "There are more things in heaven and earth . . . than are dreamt of in your philosophy" (Act 1, Scene 5). Toward the end of the play, Laertes professes that after Ophelia's death, "a ministering angel shall my sister be" (Act 5, Scene 1). Whatever philosophies might prevail in our times, it is certain that millions still ponder the many things and beings that may lie beyond our senses. Although Hamlet's encounter with the ghost of his father in theatrical drama may go far beyond ordinary experience, throughout the ages, and certainly still today, angels and demons are popularly regarded as more than fiction.

A Jewish Old Testament Perspective

In this chapter, we will begin to investigate the ancient biblical accounts of angels and see how modern narratives compare. It is important to state at the outset that belief in angels is reflected throughout the Old Testament and hence is deeply rooted in the Jewish tradition. It is possible that Israel developed its belief in angels in the transition from poly- to monotheism by transforming Canaanite deities into angels and divine messengers.[6] The Jewish belief in angels continues up to the present, as is evident in the role that angels have on the eve of Shabbat (Sabbath).[7] On this holiest day of the week, the presence of two ministering angels reminds participants that this special day recalls God's wonderful work at creation and thus is infused with holiness. In the Talmud (*Shabbat* 119b), Rabbi Jose the son of Judah explains the tradition in these words:

> Two ministering angels accompany man on the eve of the Sabbath from the synagogue to his home, one a good [angel] and one an evil [one]. And when he arrives home and finds the lamp burning, the table laid and the couch [bed] covered with a spread, the good angel exclaims, "May it be even thus on another Sabbath [too]," and the evil angel unwillingly responds "amen." But if not, the evil angel exclaims, "May it be even thus on another Sabbath [too]," and the good angel unwillingly responds, "amen."[8]

The traditional song *Shalom Aleichem* ("Peace be upon you") celebrates the arrival of the Shabbat on Friday evening and the role of the angels in accompanying the person home from the synagogue service. The ministering angels named in this song are "messengers of peace, messengers of the Most High."

Peace be with you, ministering angels,
    messengers of the Most High,
Messengers of the King of Kings, the Holy One,
    Blessed be He.
Come in peace, messengers of peace,
    messengers of the Most High,
Messengers of the King of Kings, the Holy One,
    Blessed be He.
Bless me with peace, messengers of peace,
    messengers of the Most High,
Messengers of the King of Kings, the Holy One,
    Blessed be He.
Go in peace, messengers of peace,
    messengers of the Most High,
Messengers of the King of Kings, the Holy One,
    Blessed be He.

In the Judeo-Christian tradition, angels come from a heavenly realm, and this easily accounts for their being depicted as lofty spiritual beings with wings. What mortals among us have never wished to have the ability to fly under our own power? Before the advent of aircraft, flying was always associated with feathered wings. (Bats were well known, of course, but they have no feathers and were creatures of the night and of darkness—not how angels were typically perceived.)

In many movies and television episodes, angels come to earth to assist human beings with an essential task. Their mission is seldom, if ever, one of solving a physical or material problem. The greatest of human aspirations is to attain our purpose in life, and at the end, to die with the dignity of knowing that we have succeeded in achieving significant lifetime goals. To a certain extent there is agreement here between dramatized quest stories in popular culture and biblical accounts of angelic interaction with humans.

In the Bible we can readily see that there is a significant purpose to human-angelic interactions and that, as a result, the humans are affected at turning points of great importance, which provide a true purpose for their lives. A significant difference between biblical accounts and those found in modern settings of movies and television, though, is that in the former angels always serve as agents of the one true God.

Most frequently, the angel visiting someone in the Bible is referred to as "the angel of the Lord." An angel first appears in Genesis chapter 16, yet this angel comes neither with a name nor a visual description. Sarai (later Sarah), wife of Abram (later Abraham), has given to her husband her handmaid, Hagar, as a concubine (a culturally accepted secondary wife), for the purpose of bearing a child, since Sarai, then in her old age, had never conceived a child. But when Hagar displays her pregnancy with such pride that Sarai feels belittled, Sarai treats Hagar harshly until Hagar runs away. Despairing of her life, Hagar encounters "the angel of the

Lᴏʀᴅ" who sends her back to Sarai with the assurance that the son she is about to bear, whom she is to call Ishmael, will be "a wild ass of a man" and will become the father of a countless multitude (Genesis 16:9–12). Muslims recognize Ishmael as the ancestor to several tribes and peoples.

Hagar's response to the angel reveals more than just her obedience. Before she returns to her overbearing mistress, she gives God a name, "El-roi," probably meaning both that she has seen God and lived (see Genesis 16:13), and that God has seen her and given her the protection she needs in her time of trouble. This is the first time in the Bible that the appearance of angels to humans is identified with the person of God. Two chapters later, three "men" appear at Abraham and Sarah's tent. Their arrival is also said to be a personal appearance of God:

> The Lᴏʀᴅ appeared to Abraham by the oaks of Mamre, as he sat at the entrance of his tent in the heat of the day. He looked up and saw three men standing near him. When he saw them, he ran from the tent entrance to meet them, and bowed down to the ground. (Genesis 18:1–2)

In addition to offering water to wash their feet and bread to refresh them, Abraham goes to great lengths to provide hospitality (18:4–8).

In a passage on mutual love reminiscent of Abraham's welcome, the writer of the Letter to the Hebrews instructs believers not to neglect "to show hospitality to strangers, for by doing that some have entertained angels without knowing it" (13:2). Dorothy Day, who embraced Catholicism and devoted her life to serving the poor and the homeless, believed that every guest who came to a Catholic Worker house was to be received as an angel.[9] Perhaps this conviction can change our perception of the next homeless person we pass by on the street.

As the Genesis narrative continues, it becomes evident that only one of the visiting figures is God. The other two heavenly beings are often interpreted to be angels. Although angels are spiritual beings, in this meeting all three seem to have physical bodies and sit down with Abraham to share a meal. But did they really eat and drink, or just seem to, as did the angel who said to Tobit and his son, "Although you were watching me, I really did not eat or drink anything— but what you saw was a vision" (Tobit 12:19)?

Christians down through the centuries have seen the trio who appear to Abraham as setting the stage for the doctrinal understanding of God as a Trinity of Persons— which was first explicitly proclaimed before the ecumenical councils of Nicaea (325 AD) and Constantinople (381 AD). This is exactly how St. Augustine of Hippo (354–430) interpreted Abraham's mysterious encounter.

The early fifteenth-century Russian iconographer Andrei Rublev depicted the three figures who met with Abraham in perhaps the most famous of all icons. In his portrayal, Rublev transforms the hospitality of Abraham into a representation of the Trinity, giving rise to the three "men" being referred to as "the Old Testament Trinity." With remarkable clarity, grace, and illumination, this icon portrays three winged persons with halos sitting at a table holding a cup. A common interpretation identifies the three figures from left to right as the Father, Son, and Holy Spirit. The circular flow suggested by the tilting of their heads indicates an inner harmony and unity.

Scripture scholars affirm that the importance of this angelic appearance to Abraham and Sarah is the interpretative key to a narrative that qualifies Abraham and Sarah's offspring as the chosen people of God, eventually to be known as Israel. Indeed, the purpose of the three angelic visitors is to announce to Abraham that Sarah is now to conceive their son who will be called Isaac (which means laughter):

> [The angels] said to him, "Where is your wife Sarah?" And he said, "There, in the tent." Then one said, "I will surely return to you in due season, and your wife Sarah shall have a son." And Sarah was listening at the tent entrance behind him. Now Abraham and Sarah were old, advanced in age; it had ceased to be with Sarah after the manner of women. So Sarah laughed to herself, saying, "After I have grown old, and my husband is old, shall I have pleasure?" The LORD said to Abraham, "Why did Sarah laugh, and say, 'Shall I indeed bear a child, now that I am old?' Is anything too wonderful for the LORD? At the set time I will return to you, in due season, and Sarah shall have a son." (Genesis 18:9–14)

In the Book of Exodus, an angel of the Lord makes a dramatic appearance to Moses at Horeb, the mountain of God: "There the angel of the LORD appeared to him in a flame of fire out of a bush; he looked, and the bush was blazing, yet it was not consumed" (Exodus 3:2). Usually, the angel of God appears in human form as we saw with Abraham, but this one takes the form of a blazing fire—an insubstantial yet dangerous and powerful, illuminating and purifying force. Moses stood on holy ground; he hid his face, for seeing the Divine would be too awesome to survive.

Later the biblical narrative recounts how the people of Israel returned to the land of Canaan—which Abraham's God, long before their time in Egypt, had promised to give them—and how they struggled to survive there in the dominant presence of enemies (the native people of the land). In this context, "the angel of the LORD" makes another appearance and announces once more the forthcoming birth of a child, Samson, to his mother, who like Sarah was thought to be barren.

> There was a certain man of Zorah, of the tribe of the Danites, whose name was Manoah. His wife was barren, having borne no children. And the angel of the LORD appeared to the woman and said to her, "Although you are barren, having borne no children, you shall conceive and bear a son." . . . Then the woman came and told her husband, "A man of God came to me, and his appearance was like that of an angel of God, most awe-inspiring; I did not ask him where he came

from, and he did not tell me his name; but he said to me, 'You shall conceive and bear a son.'" (Judges 13:2–3,6–7a)

The "angel of the Lord" appears to the woman in the form of a man, but not just any man. He was like "an angel of God, most awe-inspiring." Modern readers struggle with this passage for other reasons: the woman's husband is named, but not the woman herself, even though she is the more important character! Surely, she deserves to be remembered, but without a name it is difficult to remember her directly. Concerning the identity of the angel, however, there is no suggestion in this passage that the angel might be anyone other than God.

Angels and Our Salvation

What does the Bible tell us about the role of angels in handing down the covenant? As Sacred Scripture was received, edited, and passed on to succeeding generations, a tension developed between different traditions regarding the covenant promulgated through the prophet Moses. In Exodus we read that God spoke directly with Moses, without a mediator (Exodus 33:11a). But by the time the Letter to the Hebrews was written (between 60 and 100 AD), an alternative tradition had developed. Hebrews seems to reflect what became a standard belief, namely that God's covenant was revealed to Moses by angels on Mount Sinai, not by direct revelation (see Hebrews 2:2). By this time God is seldom depicted as having direct interpersonal contact with humans; instead, God is portrayed as employing angels as intermediaries, who appear bearing the power and presence of God.

In Hebrews angels are said to be spirits sent by God to reinforce God's intention to save humankind: "Are not all angels spirits in the divine service, sent to serve for the sake of those who are to inherit salvation?" (1:14). As we have seen, the word *angel* literally means "messenger." When the angel of the Lord speaks in Scripture, the angel is, in effect, the word or voice of God. As spirits they make God present in the message they bear. To hear and accept their message is to acknowledge God's presence and authority.

As helpful to humans as many fictional angels are portrayed to be in movies and television, they lack some of the strategic importance of those found in the Bible. The unnamed angel of the Lord, for example, who appears to Joseph in a dream in Matthew 1:20–23, and others such as Gabriel in Luke 1:11-20, 26-38, bear messages that radically alter the lives and perspectives of their recipients and affect the lives of succeeding generations. As we have seen, the angels' messages to Abraham and Sarah and to the wife of Manoah are promises of wellbeing which implicate all God's people. The angels' messages, when taken to heart, are meant to inform those who welcome them that God has favored their lives.

The preeminent message that angels bring in the Bible is to shepherds tending their flock: Jesus the Messiah has been born. Immediately after this, "a multitude of the heavenly host"—a term meaning group or army (see "host of angels" in 2 Esdras 6:3, 8:21)—suddenly appears, breaking out in praise to the Divine: "Glory to God in the highest heaven, / and on earth peace among those whom he favors!" (Luke 2:14). Have you ever wondered who tended the sheep when the shepherds left their flocks and went to see the Christ Child lying in the manger? This query prompted a children's author to create a story about a young boy who is asked to stay and mind the sheep. But then the Angel Gabriel returns and takes the boy on a mystical flight to be the first to witness the Christmas miracle.[10]

Once the adult Jesus begins his ministry, we learn that he, too, is attended to by angels. Mark tells us most succinctly that after his baptism, Jesus "was in the wilderness forty days, tempted by Satan; and he was with the wild beasts; and the angels waited on him" (1:13). Here angels assist Jesus in a time of trial. In John's Gospel we hear Jesus tell his newest follower, Nathanael, "Very truly, I tell you, you will see heaven opened and the angels of God ascending and descending upon the Son of Man" (1:51). Yet we are not told of any announcement the angels delivered in these instances. They are sent to minister to Jesus, but any message of spiritual or theological importance comes not from an angel but directly from the mouth of Jesus. However important angels were to announcing God's saving activity up until and including the birth of Jesus, the New Testament consistently places subsequent messages concerning God's plan of salvation in the words and deeds of human beings, preeminently those of Jesus but also of the people called by him, namely the apostles.

In the Acts of the Apostles, the signal event that marks the message of salvation as intended for not just the Jewish people, but Gentiles as well, happens in the story of Cornelius (chapter 10). The interaction between the Roman centurion Cornelius, who worshipped the God of the Jews, and a reluctant Peter, who initially balked at the universal claim of God's message, is dramatic and unveils far-reaching implications. Cornelius apparently knew nothing about the messianic movement being led by Jesus' followers (the foremost of whom was Peter) until an angel appeared to him and informed him that his devotion to God was about to be rewarded. He was to send for Peter, who was staying in Joppa, nearly 40 miles distant. Meanwhile Peter received a vision which he interpreted to mean that God had now accepted Gentiles as well as Jews for his people. Cornelius's messengers brought Peter to him and it was Peter, not an angel, who proclaimed the good news of salvation in Jesus to Cornelius and his household.

In the New Testament another designation related to the word *angel*, in addition to "messenger," is "apostle": a person sent to bear the message of salvation. Jesus affirms that the apostles "will be my witnesses in Jerusalem, throughout Judea and Samaria, and to the ends of the earth" (Acts 1:8). As wondrous as it might seem to be visited by angels, the apostolic witness to Jesus Christ found in Scripture carries even greater significance for us.

Angels in the Gospels

Let's go back for a moment and take a closer look at where angels make their appearance in the life and mission of Jesus. In the Gospel of Luke, for example, an angel or angels play a prominent role in four key events in the life of Jesus: his conception and birth, his death, his resurrection, and his return at the end of time. An angel announces to a young and unsuspecting woman that she will bear a son (Luke 1:26–38) and later an angel tells nearby shepherds that the Messiah has been born (2:8–13); an angel strengthens Jesus in his anguish just prior to his excruciating death (22:43-44, absent in some manuscripts); angels appear to perplexed women at the tomb telling them that Jesus, who had been buried in the tomb, was now alive (24:23, see also "two men in dazzling clothes" in 24:4-5); angels are to accompany and to witness to the Son of Man when he returns and witness to the fidelity of believers (9:26, 12:8–9). Angels served as messenger and comforter, interpreter and witness at three crucial times during the life of Jesus and they will again at his return.

Notice that angels do not make an appearance at Jesus' baptism or Transfiguration, for at these seminal events the speaker is the very person of God, who declares to Jesus at his baptism: "You are my Son, the Beloved; with you I am well pleased" (Luke 3:22) and similarly at his Transfiguration: "This is my Son, my Chosen" (9:35). All attention is on the authority of the divine voice and the unique and intimate relationship between Father and Son.

Angels are not intended to take center stage but to serve as messengers of the divine plan.

In the Gospel of Matthew, Jesus expands on the role of angels in his return at the end of time. In the parable of the weeds and the wheat (13:24–30, 36–43), Jesus compares the kingdom of heaven to someone who has sowed good seed in his field. An enemy sows weeds among the good seed, but the sower tells his workers to wait until the harvest to remove them, so they don't uproot the wheat with the weeds. Jesus explains to his disciples:

> "The one who sows the good seed is the Son of Man; the field is the world, and the good seed are the children of the kingdom; the weeds are the children of the evil one, and the enemy who sowed them is the devil; the harvest is the end of the age, and the reapers are angels." (12:37-39)

He goes on to explain that "at the end of the age" he will send his angels to gather "all causes of sin and all evildoers" and throw them out of his kingdom. "Then the righteous will shine like the sun in the kingdom of their Father" (verse 43). A similar parable appears in Matthew 13:47–50: Just as fishermen sort good fish from bad after hauling in their nets, so the angels "will come out and separate the evil from the righteous" at the end of time.

One of the most well known passages in Matthew is "The Judgment of the Nations" (25:31-46). Jesus begins, "When the Son of Man comes in his glory, and all the angels with him, then he will sit on the throne of his glory."

In describing the last judgment, when "all the nations will be gathered before him," Jesus tells us, "just as you did it to one of the least of these who are members of my family, you did it to me." The acts of service that we do (or do not do) for "the least of these" have become known as the corporal works of mercy. The angels are present at Jesus' side in his glory, and they will witness his judgment of all human beings.

The angels, who already made the definitive choice to follow God (just as demons, fallen angels, made the definitive choice not to follow God), will be witnesses to the results of our choices in life, whether we followed God or chose evil. They too are part of God's creation and his plan. As fully good and purely spiritual beings, angels are tasked with bringing righteous human beings into the kingdom at the end of time, where they can live forever unhindered by evil influences.

When we look at the resurrection accounts in all four Gospels (Matthew 28:1–10; Mark 16:1–14; Luke 24:1–12,30–41; John 20:11–18), we see that angels are once again present as messengers, pointing the witnesses to the reality of Jesus' resurrection, instead of taking center stage themselves. Rather, the women's and the disciples' encounters with the risen Lord are the important events in these accounts. And after Jesus' Ascension (Acts 1:6–11), angels appear to the disciples to remind them to attend to their new mission as Jesus' witnesses "to the ends of the earth."

Contemporary Interest in Angels and Demons

What is it that draws our imagination to, or even encourages our belief in, angels? Is it the desire to close the gap between heaven and earth? Is it an amorphous fear of the unknown that lets us posit demons, or is it something more specific and pernicious, such as the fear of evil itself?

To answer these questions, we need only recall some prevailing themes in movies, books, and television about angels. These media have endeavored to give us novel approaches to a subject that is actually quite ancient. Angels are anything but new, yet interest in them is never stale or tiresome. But in providing us with a fresh take on something so embedded in our culture and history, celluloid angels and the like also bring into popular understanding elements that contrast with what the Bible—an enduring cultural as well as religious narrative—says concerning angels.

How we conjecture about angels and demons can influence our understanding of what it means to be human in a creation much larger than ourselves, one that stretches far beyond what we can grasp with our senses. In popular culture, angels have altered significantly from their appearance in biblical literature. Briefly exploring modern treatments of angels can be revealing, even though the biblical accounts of angelic presences have something more significant to say about them.

Forty years after his death, the character Jonathan Smith reappeared in *Highway to Heaven* as an angel. His wings, however, were never quite visible as he hitchhiked down the road. The opening scene of the five-season hit (1984–1989) is blurred just enough to give us a cloudy impression of someone whose full head of flouncy hair might actually be a halo and whose arms, in the puffed shoulders of his bulky jacket, might really be backed by wings.

Almost all of us know that when the bell chimed on the Christmas tree in the perennial holiday favorite *It's a Wonderful Life* (1946), the probationary angel Clarence had finally earned his wings. Clarence had intervened in the life of George Bailey, dissuading him from suicide. The unexpected angelic mediator bridged the gap between heaven and earth to make a profound change in one man's life and in the lives of the people that man encountered. This theme of angelic intervention is taken up in several subsequent films and TV series.

Hollywood knows what we expect from angels, even as it seeks to surprise us by their interactions with us mortals. In the 1996 film *Michael*, starring John Travolta as an improbable angel, the very earthy and foible-filled title character has his true identity as an angel exposed when a stray feather pokes out from under his earthly garb. It is certainly a cultural standard that angels should have wings, but the fantastical creatures bearing wings in the Bible are usually depicted as attendants to God on his heavenly throne, such as the six-winged seraphim (Isaiah 6:2) or as the carved images of cherubim that surround God's seat above the ark of the covenant (Exodus 37:9)—not as the mesengers sent to human beings.

The association of messenger angels with wings probably has more to do with the age-old understanding of the transcendent nature of angels as heavenly beings rather than with any biblical evidence. Those that appear in Genesis to Abraham and Isaac, for example, lack these appendages. With or without wings, angels come from above, and "above" at one time always meant beyond us, up in the sky, where heaven was understood to be. Thus, according to the common imagination, angels would naturally be creatures of the sky, flying high above the earth.

In addition to consistent depictions of angels with wings, Hollywood's angels often have an earthier side, one that involves them in human affairs. In fact, angels are regularly portrayed as the souls of humans blessed with a heavenly life after death. In the biblical perspective, however, the radical transformation of the physical body of human beings—a prerequisite for the life to come—into a spiritual body is called the resurrection (see 1 Corinthians chapter 15). Human beings are raised from the dead as glorified human bodies; we do not become angels, who are pure spirit.

Common Themes

In popular culture there is no single, universal agreement concerning the nature of angels. Angels are easily left to the imagination. Although they are both imagined and imaged in many ways—often reflecting biblical themes—there are some common sentiments in their pop culture representations:

1. Angels come from a heavenly realm beyond space and time, a realm that is understood more spiritually than ours. In modern narratives God is often alluded to but is rarely a central figure.

2. Angels regularly appear as humans without wings, as in much of biblical literature.

3. Angels are typically agents of goodwill who interact with humans, often for an important spiritual purpose. This purpose is usually meant to benefit one or more human beings and perhaps has significance for the angel as well.

4. Occasionally, angels are departed human spirits returning to earth to rectify something lacking completion or fulfillment in their mortal life.

5. In some modern and ancient narratives, angels, though exclusively spiritual in nature, desire the sensual experiences available only to incarnate (human) beings.

6. Dark, fallen angels—collectively associated with the devil and other demons—were created naturally good by God but by their own doing became evil. These seek to wreak havoc and chaos in the world of human relations.

In this chapter we focused on the unique role of angels as messengers of the divine in the lives of Hagar, Abraham and Sarah, the unnamed woman in Judges, Jesus and his followers, and Peter and Cornelius. While angels retain their role as messengers and ministers in the New Testament, the unique role of human beings—namely Jesus and subsequently the apostles—takes center stage. Through their words and deeds, they proclaim God's message of salvation to their fellow human beings. We also reviewed the fascination with angelic beings in contemporary media and summarized their main characteristics and functions. In the next chapter we will continue to look closely at biblical encounters with individual angels, some of whom are named.

For Reflection

- What is your own opinion about the existence of angels? Do you believe they interact with human beings? Have you ever encountered one?

- Based on your experience of modern depictions of angels in media, what kind of messages do they bear? Are these messages important or attractive to you?

Chapter Two

Angels Ascending and Descending

Have you ever encountered an angel? I mean an actual angel, not a kind human being who did something nice for you and thus was perceived metaphorically as "a real angel." A deeper question might be, do you believe that angels and human beings interact? If you have followed television shows in recent decades, you would think there was regular contact between angels and humans, virtually on a daily basis. Fictional angels manifest themselves not just at Christmas, but year-round, and not just to Christians, but to those from a broad spectrum of perspectives, including non-believers.

In this chapter we will examine the phenomenon of angelic interactions with humans a little more carefully from a biblical perspective. We start with a passage in the Gospel of John, where Jesus assured Nathanael that he would see angels ascending and descending on the "Son of Man" (a self-identifying title referring to Jesus; John 1:51). This dynamic interaction between the earth and the world above is reminiscent of the patriarch Jacob's dream in which he sees heaven open and angels ascending and descending on a ladder that connects heaven and earth (Genesis 28:10–17). In John's Gospel, Jesus tells Nathanael that if he follows Jesus, he will discover that Jesus is himself the ladder, namely, the link, between heaven and earth.

A Modern Perspective

In popular culture today, angels are metaphorically cast as ascending and descending, but not necessarily as ministering spirits like those Nathanael was told he would see.

Today, what is often depicted as the ascension of angels is actually their rising to greater responsibility and authority in the heavenly realm. Angels are occasionally thought of as departed humans, who, having arrived in heaven, now must be trained as angels, perhaps even passing through several progressive stages. The descent of angels can mean anything from a fall into perdition, to a literal crash into earth, to an eager return into mortal human flesh.

The TV series *Touched by an Angel* (1994–2003) eventually revealed a deep backstory for the angel Monica, portrayed by Irish actress Roma Downey. Monica progressively trained for various angelic positions. She began in an angelic choir, then went on to rapid-response rescues of distraught humans, before being mentored by Tess (Della Reese). This angelic social worker was sent to positively influence the lives of various human individuals caught in the throes of complex personal crises, whether physical or emotional. These crises formed the basis of each episode.

The plot lines featuring Monica's angelic involvement in human ordeals vary little from those in *Highway to*

Heaven, in which Michael Landon plays the once-human, now-probationary-angel Jonathan Smith. By means both miraculous and mundane, these angels foster in their human assignments the courage needed to confront and overcome the challenges they face.

As these once-human denizens of earth learn to live out their newly acquired heavenly status as angels, their contact with humans still living on earth brings about positive changes for the people with whom they engage. Whether we accept them as definitive representations of actual angels or not, the depictions reinforce a cultural perception of angels as agents of God—divine "helpers," really—sent to promote goodness and happiness among human beings.

There remains, however, something essentially human in the duties and heavenly progression of these fictional angels. They still need to learn and to grow from what they experience through their encounters with ordinary humans. The "good" angels we encounter in modern media come with a reassuring message: no matter how challenging our life is, even when we are confronted with the fact of our own mortality, we can learn from experience and mature as long as we embrace the fact that our life has purpose.

A Biblical Perspective

The stories we hear about humanizing angels tell us more about ourselves than they do about angels. How then can we know anything about angels for sure? Traditionally angels are defined as heavenly beings, spirits who take on human-like characteristics when necessary. Such portrayals bring us closer to biblical encounters with angels than modern stories. In Scripture, angels are messengers who seldom make more than cameo appearances.

An exception is the prolonged appearance of and assistance provided by the angel Raphael in the Book of Tobit (probably written in the second century BC). It offers the most extended and detailed description of an angel's activities in the entire Bible. Dramatically emphasizing God's care for people in extremely difficult circumstances, this book tells about an Israelite couple (Tobit and Anna) and their son (Tobias) during the time of exile in Nineveh, following the Assyrian destruction of Israel and the subsequent scattering of its peoples to foreign lands.

Tobit is a faithful servant of God, obedient to the Mosaic Law. He defies the orders of several successive emperors by secretly burying the bodies of his fellow Israelites whom these rulers had slain in persecution. Following one last burial which made him ritually impure due to handling the corpse, Tobit sleeps outside in order not to defile his household. But birds drop their excrement on his eyes before he wakes, and when he does, he discovers he is blind. His wife Anna must go to work in order to support them, which shames Tobit. He has, however, an alternative: contact Gabel, a relative far outside Nineveh has has been keeping Tobit's fortune of silver safe. Tobit sends his son Tobias to reclaim it, and at the same time, charges him to find and marry a faithful kinswoman.

Into this story Raphael enters as a principal character who only reveals his identity as an angel later in the narrative (Tobit 12:15). His mission to earth is succinctly announced: "So Raphael was sent [by God] to heal" (3:17)—this is the only time God is the subject of an action in the book—and more generally "to work" (5:5). In addition to healing, Raphael's task is to bring success to the lives of Tobit, his son Tobias, and Sarah, Tobias's bride-to-be. Raphael is a flawless superhero who needs to undergo none of the character development that modern renditions of superheroes experience. Disguised as a young man, Raphael functions in multiple ways as a messenger: from God to humans, from humans to God, and between humans. He serves as a guide and protector (5:4–5); offers encouragement to Tobit (5:10); acts as marriage broker between Tobias and Sarah (6:11–16); invites Gabael to Tobias's wedding feast (9:5); announces to Tobias his father's healing (11:7); and brings the prayers of Tobit and Sarah "before the Glory of the Lord" (12:12).

It is worth noting that Raphael is not himself the healer—as he is primarily known—but rather a medical advisor, instructing Tobias on how to heal his father's blindness. Thus Raphael, continuing to act as a messenger between God and humans, facilitates divine healing. Tobias is to remove the gall, heart, and liver from the fish he caught, use the heart and liver to drive away evil spirits, and smear the gall on the eyes of his blind father to restore his sight (6:5–9; 11:4,7–8). The latter reflects the medical practice for healing blindness in the second century BC.[11]

The book of First Enoch, written a few centuries after Tobit, singles out Raphael as the angel "who is set over all disease and every wound of the children of the people" (40:9).[12] How fitting then that Raphael is called upon for healing in this traditional prayer:

> O Glorious Archangel St. Raphael, great prince of the heavenly court, you are illustrious for your gifts of wisdom and grace. You are a guide of those who journey by land or sea or air, consoler of the afflicted, and refuge of sinners. I beg you, assist me in all my needs and in all the sufferings of this life, as once you helped the young Tobias on his travels. Because you are the "medicine of God" I humbly pray you to heal the many infirmities of my soul and the ills that afflict my body. . . . Amen.[13]

Besides Raphael, only two other angels, Michael and Gabriel, are identified by name in the Bible. Michael is introduced in the Book of Daniel as a great and future prince of God's people, who shall arise and announce victory for the oppressed through resurrection to everlasting life (Daniel 12:1–4). Michael is also named in Jude verse 9 as an archangel, and in Revelation 12:7–9 as the one commanding the angels who successfully wage war against Satan.

Gabriel appears and speaks twice in Daniel (8:16–26 and 9:21–27) to explain Daniel's visions to him and twice again in Luke (1:11–20 and 1:26–38) as the one who announces the conceptions of John the Baptist and Jesus. Even though these three angels are named, they, with the possible exception of Raphael, are not revealed to us as self-directed persons in the way that humans function. They always appear in the context of a mission and thus are indistinguishable from their mission. Their names all end in *-el*, meaning "God" in Hebrew. Hence, *Raphael* means "God's healing"; *Michael* means "the face of God," or "who is like God?"; and *Gabriel* refers to "the might" or "strength" of God. Raphael is sent to heal, Michael confronts the enemies of the divine, and Gabriel announces God's powerful intervention in human affairs.

How many angels there are in total is anyone's guess. Tobit identifies Raphael as one of seven (Tobit 12:15); First Enoch names six archangels, each with its own function (1 Enoch chapter 20). The most developed hierarchy of angels comes from Pseudo-Dionysius (a theologian who lived in the late fifth to early sixth century AD), who describes three orders with three ranks each: the highest order (seraphim, cherubim, thrones), the middle order (dominions, virtues, powers), and the lowest order (principles, archangels, angels). Personal guardian angels are included in the last category. Known in the Catholic Church as the nine choirs of angels and mentioned by several saints throughout Christian history, each of these designations is found in scattered references throughout the Bible.[14] Some believers have found these angels, ranked with particular qualities, to be helpful sources of inspiration in their spiritual life.

In Broader Perspective

Unlike so many other depictions of angels in film and literature, the Christian apologist C. S. Lewis captures well the authentic biblical sense of angelic presence in the books of his *Space Trilogy* (published in 1938, 1943, and 1945). In *Perelandra*, the second novel, Dr. Ransom, the protagonist, asks the narrator (presumptively Lewis) to meet him in his cottage. The narrator is a bit hesitant, since he knows Ransom has been in contact with *eldila*, described as powerful extraterrestrial angelic figures who inhabit deep space. When the narrator enters Ransom's cottage, he is immediately aware of an overwhelming presence of spiritual goodness. This unnerves him, for he senses that such powerful goodness does not necessarily mean good things for him. This is Lewis's allegorical way of stating that humans are subject to original sin—they are flawed and subject to temptation, particularly the temptation to power.

Ascending and Descending

The lives of angels and humans can and do intersect. There is indeed descending and ascending; there is intercourse between heaven and earth. This interchange is demonstrated most profoundly in the infancy narratives of Matthew and Luke.

In these two Gospels angels of great authority announce momentous births and provide life-saving guidance. An angel of the Lord appears in a dream and instructs a perplexed Joseph to take Mary as his wife, for she will bear a child by the Holy Spirit. The child will eventually be given a theological name: Emmanuel ("God with us"), because he is the very Incarnation of the Divine. Notice that Joseph accepts and never questions the heavenly origin of the one who appears in his dream. Later, the angel directs Joseph—again through a dream—to save the life of this child by fleeing to Egypt, and, once more in a dream, informs him when it is safe to return to the land of Israel (Matthew 1:20,24; 2:13,19–20).

Through the centuries, angels have appeared in dreams offering guidance and comfort. By meeting with a trained spiritual director, persons who have such experiences can discern how God may be at work in their life offering direction and clarity, for example, about perplexing situations.

In Luke's Gospel, as we have seen, an angel appeared to a terrified Zechariah who was performing his priestly service in the sanctuary of the Temple, informing him that his elderly wife would bear a son. Later in the dialogue this angel identifies himself as Gabriel and states his credentials: "I stand in the presence of God, and I have been sent . . . to bring you this good news" (1:8–20). Gabriel next appears to Mary, announcing that she has found favor with God and will conceive a son to be called Jesus. She questions how this will happen, since she is a virgin. Then, after the angel elaborates the unusual circumstances to unfold, Mary makes a firm commitment to embrace God's plan (1:26–38).

Responding to Fear

One theme that runs through the angelic encounters with Joseph, Zechariah, and Mary, as well as other biblical appearances from celestial messengers, is fear. When the angel of God appears to a troubled Hagar, the angel instructs her "Do not be afraid" for God has heard her son's voice (Genesis 21:17). Similarly, an angel counsels a bewildered Joseph to not be afraid (Matthew 1:20). Zechariah is terrified, and the visiting angel offers the same instruction (Luke 1:13). Literally translated, Mary is "very terrified" by the angel's words, perhaps by the very appearance of the angel, and so the angel comforts her: "Do not be afraid" (Luke 1:29–30). And once again the angels bring this now familiar refrain to startled humans, namely the shepherds in the field: "Do not be afraid" (Luke 2:10).

Throughout the Bible the human response to angelic and divine presence is fear. Often when God appears in dramatic theophanies that display awesome power, God counsels humans not to be afraid (Genesis 15:1, 26:24; Revelation 1:17). Similarly, Jesus regularly reminds his frightened and anxious followers not to fear, particularly when he has demonstrated his power as the Son of God (Matthew 14:27, Luke 5:10). The experience of the Divine and divine emissaries is far beyond any human encounter. The response to the transcendent is thus unspeakable awe, called by the Danish theologian Søren Kierkegaard (1813–1855) *mysterium tremendum et fascinans*: an encounter that is both terrifying and fascinating.

During one winter, the Austrian poet Rainer Maria Rilke (1875–1926) reported hearing the voice of an angel while walking along the cliffs in Trieste on the Adriatic Sea. An angel appeared to him and spoke about life and death, inspiring him to write the *Duino Elegies*, in which he grapples with the loneliness of human beings in the universe. He asks: "Who, if I cried out, would hear me among the angels' hierarchies?" Calling upon angels to notice and respond to human suffering, he has a momentary, frightening experience of beauty "which we are barely able to endure." Overwhelmed with such unspeakable splendor, he portrayed this magnificence through the symbol of an angel who represents a perfection beyond all human limitations. Because of their astounding beauty, he exclaims, reminiscent of Kierkegaard, "each single angel is terrifying."[15]

Between Heaven and Earth

There is another popular narrative concerning angels, namely those that portray humans as having greater influence on the lives of angels than vice versa. These are not stories of divinely empowered rescues by once-human angels intent on rising to a higher calling, but of depraved fallenness, including angels lured by the intoxicating possibilities inherent in human sensuality. It might surprise many to learn that the theme of fallen angels has more biblical support than the notion that after death humans will become angels (which has none).

The theme of fallen angels recurs throughout the centuries. "Lucifer"—meaning "light bearer" or "shining one" in both Hebrew and Latin—is a moniker attached to the angel otherwise known as Satan, the crown prince of evil. "Lucifer" is the translation found in the King James Version and the Douay Rheims (Catholic) Bible of the fallen mighty power in Isaiah 14:12: "How art thou fallen from heaven, O Lucifer, son of the morning! how art thou cut down to the ground, which didst weaken the nations!" Most modern English versions translate the name instead as "morning star" (NIV) or "Day Star" (NRSV, NABRE). Historically, the planet Venus was considered the morning star, or day star. Because Venus, called "Lucifer" in Latin, disappeared from view regularly, the planet was said to have fallen from the heavens.

Many biblical scholars regard this "Day Star" in Isaiah 14:12 as a reference to a defeated and deceased Babylonian emperor. In a taunting dirge, Isaiah contrasts Lucifer's sealed fate with his once-tremendous victories, including the destruction of the kingdom of Judah. In the New Testament, the fallen star is identified with Satan, as is evident in Jesus' words to the disciples, who discover the power they possess over evil forces by employing Jesus' name: "I watched Satan fall from heaven like a flash of lightning" (Luke 10:18). It was only centuries after Christ that Lucifer was associated with Satan (to be discussed in chapter four).

The notion of humans falling from the celestial sphere where they once dwelt is reflected in the gnostic gospels—from the Greek *gnosis*, "secret knowledge"—

discovered in 1945 near the village of Nag Hammadi in Egypt. The authors of these texts held that humans were once spiritual, angelic beings who became imprisoned in flesh by the wicked "god" responsible for earthly, material creation. Christ was thought by many gnostics to be a liberating spirit who used the body of Jesus to teach the way to spiritual freedom from the flesh. He allegedly taught humans to pursue secret, hidden knowledge (*gnosis*) that would lead to liberation from the prison of human flesh and to ultimate enlightenment, resulting in their return to the heavenly sphere. It should be noted that this conception of the spiritual and material aspects of human beings as fundamentally opposed to one another is incompatible with Christian Scriptures and beliefs.

An older tradition of spiritual beings becoming entangled in the wiles of the flesh occurs in Genesis 6:1–4. There, we encounter angels who are attracted to women. This passage recounts that in the days before the flood, there were angelic beings ("the sons of God") who lusted after the beautiful daughters born to human beings. So, crossing boundaries, they came to earth and had intercourse with them, producing offspring who came to be known as giants, powerful warriors called Nephilim, "heroes that were of old" (Genesis 6:4).

An expanded version of this event appears in 1 Enoch 6:1–2:

> In those days, when the children of man had multiplied, it happened that there were born unto

them handsome and beautiful daughters. And the angels, the children of the heaven, saw them and desired them; and they said to one another, "Come, let us choose wives for ourselves from among the daughters of man and beget us children."[16]

The narrative continues a few chapters later:

Then [the good angelic watchers] Michael, Surafel, and Gabriel observed carefully from the sky and they saw much blood being shed upon the earth, and all the oppression being wrought upon the earth. And they said one to another, "The earth (from) her empty (foundation) has brought the cry of their voice into the gates of heaven." (9:1-2)[17]

The Most High then brought judgment upon the people by destroying all on earth through a deluge and by having Raphael the archangel cast into darkness Asael, the corrupt ringleader of the fallen angels. Much like the warring superheroes of *Watchmen*, the good and evil watchers in First Enoch battled for the future of humankind.

From this mythological episode, these mighty figures and their angelic progenitors have stoked our imagination for centuries. In modern terms, they would be considered supervillains. While the stories we tell over the millenia may differ in their religious intent, their characters and plots are similar. Characteristically, superheroes, supervillains, and their rivalries embroil mortal humans in cosmic conflagrations.

The angelic spirits mentioned in Genesis 6:4 also surface in the Letter of Jude (verse 6), where their punishment is to be "kept in eternal chains in deepest darkness" (see also 2 Peter 2:4 where the sinful angels are cast into hell). Jude 14–15 quotes a version of 1 Enoch 1:9 which promises that the Lord is coming to execute judgment.

Enoch, the subject and traditionally the writer of the apocryphal books bearing his name, is mentioned in Genesis: "Enoch walked with God after the birth of Methuselah three hundred years, and had other sons and daughters. . . . Enoch walked with God; then he was no more, because God took him" (5:22,24). The prevailing tradition is that Enoch was taken directly up into heaven by God. In First Enoch, he is portrayed as revealing a great deal about the cause of evil and strife among humans. Human history is depicted as a cosmic battle between good and evil. The evil is perpetrated by those angels who came down to earth and consorted with the female descendants of Adam, who bore them children. These children wage war on the rest of the human race. In Enoch, the evil angels are known as "the watchers," whose duties included spying on the activities of humans on earth. Much like Satan in the Book of Job, they were supposed to keep God informed of human behavior, whether good or evil, but many of the watchers themselves became evil and sowed even more evil among humankind. The cosmic war between good and evil angels depicted in Enoch is echoed in the canonical Book of Revelation which portrays in vivid imagery the dramatic conflict between the Cosmic Christ and the Satanic beast.

In this chapter we have explored the theme of angels ascending and descending between heaven and earth. Also, we have seen that in popular culture humans can often become angels after death, with the possibility for endless growth and achievement. In movies angels yearn for the sensate richness of romantic love that belongs, apparently, only to humans. This theme is not new, as we have seen by looking at passages in Scripture and First Enoch where angelic beings lust for women. In the gnostic tradition it was believed that angels were trapped in a human body (an analogous belief that persists today among some religious fringe groups). Finally, we explored how being in the presence of God and the angels is an awe-inspiring experience that can prove unnerving, even terrifying, in part because of the power and mission given to the angels by God. The world of demons also evokes fear but of a radically different kind, and to that world we now turn.

For Reflection

- What modern depictions of angels are you familiar with? What have you found most appealing about these portrayals?

- What similarities do you see between biblical encounters with angels and non-biblical descriptions? What differences between them are significant to you?

Chapter Three

Wrestling with Demons

Often we associate thoughts of angels or of anything "angelic" with a person's goodness or with someone whose very being radiates a benevolent, helpful spirit. But there is a darker side. Stories in the Bible and beyond bring to us accounts of spiritual beings with a far different, tenaciously evil presence. These are called demons. Sometimes the term is tossed about lightly, for example, when we call a person who gets behind the wheel to drive as fast as possible a "speed demon."

The Origin of Demons

The ancient notion of a demon (from the Greek *daimōn*) was not exclusively negative, but could refer to any powerful spirit, good or bad. Today, we might speak of a variety of demons. Anyone who pursues any object or goal with a feverish, single-minded intensity might be referred to metaphorically as a demon, for example "a demon for work." Normally, however, demons are most often thought of as beings of pure evil. While many today might doubt the reality of demons, our fantasies seem to require them. Horror stories and movies are among the most popular and profitable entertainment genres of our time. Indeed, demons have persisted in populating our imagination for centuries. Dante's *Inferno* (1320; a part of his magnificent poetic work *The Divine Comedy*, which helped launch the Renaissance) depicted hell as a realm of nine descending circles, where sinners from bad to worse are tormented by demons for their unrepented moral failures. The horrific duty of these evil spiritual agents was to eternally torture deceased sinners according to the nature of their sins.

Humanity's belief in demons has a long history, going back to Mesopotamian and Greek mythologies. Regarding the latter, it is understood that when the first race of humans died, they became "pure spirits" (demons) who roamed the earth. They functioned as guardians and protectors of people as well as nations. Typically, these demons ranked between gods and mortals, serving as intermediaries between the two.

By contrast, belief in demons in ancient Israel seems to be nearly absent, since the Israelites considered them to be an aspect of neighboring polytheistic religions that Israel's prophets condemned. In Deuteronomy 32:17 and Psalm 106:37—the only two specific mentions of demons in the Hebrew Bible—demons are identified as the objects of idolatrous worship; the latter passage refers to the sacrifice of children to demons. The apostle Paul also refers to idolatrous worship as that offered to demons: "what pagans sacrifice, they sacrifice to demons and not to God" (1 Corinthians 10:20). Prior to Paul, it was not until the Babylonian exile (587 BC) and the period following the rebuilding of the Second Temple in Jerusalem that demons became a significant part of Israel's religious cosmology.

In the Book of Tobit, discussed in the previous chapter, a demon by the name of Asmodeus plays a prominent, villainous role. He is the one responsible for slaying Sarah's seven husbands (3:8) before the marriage could be consummated. (This is undoubtedly the literary source behind the Sadducees' questioning of Jesus concerning remarriage and the resurrection in Mark 12:18–25.) Because of Tobit's and Sarah's faithfulness and ardent prayers, God sends to them Raphael, to heal Tobit, to protect Tobias on his journey, and to defeat the demon.

Tobit is the first book in the Bible to describe demonic exorcism. Following Raphael's instructions, Tobias exorcises the demon on his wedding night by burning the heart and liver of a large fish over incense in Sarah's bedroom. Asmodeus flees to Egypt (in biblical reference, a land of slavery) and is pursued by Raphael, who binds him "hand and foot" (Tobit 8:2–3). Foreshadowing the fierce conflict between angels and demons in subsequent biblical literature, "binding" is a powerful word indicating a type of capture that incapacitates. It does not, however, imply the death of the one bound.

While only named twice in the Hebrew Bible (excluding Tobit and the other deuterocanonical books), demons, "unclean spirits," and "demoniacs" (demon-possessed individuals) are mentioned about one hundred times in the New Testament (NRSV). What is most significant about their presence is not the degree of their activity, but of their demise. Demons by any name appear in the New Testament as personifications of evil. The Synoptic Gospels accentuate their total surrender to Jesus' authority. The only mention of demons in the Gospel of John is in accusations against Christ, that he is possessed by a demon (7:20, 8:48–52, 10:20–21).

The Devil: A Portrait

Satan or Beelzebul, Lucifer or even Old Nick (a popular English term for the devil)—the devil may go by many names. Yet, the most common image of him is hard to shake. This portrayal—a little guy with red skin, pitchfork in hand, long pointed tail, horns, and a moustache and goatee reminiscent of Vladimir Lenin—has become a cliché in Halloween costumes, advertisements for spicy foods, and cartoons where he often sits atop someone's shoulder, leading the person into temptation by whispering in their ear.

In the Bible, the devil belongs to "the cosmic powers of this present darkness" and "the spiritual forces of evil" (Ephesians 6:12). The devil is the embodiment of evil, the one who lures believers into sin, the one who convinces us to turn our backs on Christ. It takes a great deal of God's grace and courage to renounce the devil to his face.

In movies the devil sometimes appears shrouded in the smoke of what is traditionally burning brimstone. More recently, the TV series *Lucifer* depicts him as a suave, smooth-talking nightclub owner who, bored with hell, moved to Los Angeles. In popular culture, the devil is either a source of horror despoiling the lives of ordinary but flawed people or a tempter who has the power to grant a multitude of wishes—for the price of your soul. Identifying someone with the devil has even become a meme in political rhetoric. To what extent the behavior and actions of a person actually merit the designation "diabolical" is influenced not just by one's political persuasion, but also by how one appraises moral character or the lack thereof.

But is there an evil even greater than what our imaginations can conjure? Is there a deliberately malicious evil force, a personal power, that dominates or inspires the vile acts of individuals or the many maniacal human conspiracies? Does Satan exist—is there *a* devil? Along with our historical awareness of unfathomable acts of evil perpetrated by humans, contemporary society holds intertwined religious perspectives of an ancient conflict between good and evil. In the biblical explanation of this conflict, the influence that lures and tempts individuals and entire societies to eschew any semblance of conscience in order to feed lust, greed, and a host of other twisted desires is embodied in the one we call Satan.

The English term "satan" comes from the Hebrew *satan*, a word meaning "accuser," which appears in the Old Testament most frequently with the definite article ("the satan"). Hence, it is a common noun—not a proper name—meaning "the accuser." As an adversary and tester of humans, "the satan" in the Old Testament has a role similar to that of a prosecuting attorney. The term also occurs in a verbal form, where it means either "to accuse" or "to slander." In the Psalms the petitioner laments those who "for my love . . . accuse me" (109:4); identifies "adversaries" who "render me evil for good" (38:20); and prays that "my accusers be put to shame and consumed" (71:13). By repaying good with evil, these adversaries slander and thus inflict pain on those whose character they defame.

The first person referred to as "satan" in the Bible is none other than King David, whom the Philistines complained would become their "adversary" in battle (1 Samuel 29:4). Later, Solomon is said to be without an "adversary" (*satan*), that is, a military rival (1 Kings 5:4). A few decades ago, the Iranian supreme leader Ruhollah Khomeini made ample use of "satan" as a derogatory label for his military and ideological rivals, calling Israel "Little Satan," the Soviet Union "Lesser Satan," and the United States "the Great Satan."

The satan, as an angelic figure of malicious importance, is particularly prominent in the first two chapters of Job (mentioned 14 times, compared to 12 times in the rest of the Old Testament), where he appears in the divine council:

> One day the heavenly beings came to present themselves before the LORD, and Satan also came among them. The LORD said to Satan, "Where have you come from?" Satan answered the LORD, "From going to and fro on the earth, and from walking up and down on it." The LORD said to Satan, "Have you considered my servant Job?

There is no one like him on the earth, a blameless and upright man who fears God and turns away from evil." Then Satan answered the LORD, "Does Job fear God for nothing? . . . You have blessed the work of his hands, and his possessions have increased in the land. But stretch out your hand now, and touch all that he has, and he will curse you to your face." The LORD said to Satan, "Very well, all that he has is in your power; only do not stretch out your hand against him!" So Satan went out from the presence of the LORD. (Job 1:6–12)

This is a remarkable passage, since it is the only instance in the Old Testament where God dialogues with the satan. Whether the satan is an intruder or a legitimate member of the heavenly court is uncertain. In any case, the satan acts under the auspices of God's authority who, surprisingly, puts all Job has in his power. Satan then assumes the task of proving to God that Job's goodness is due only to having been lavished with much wealth and familial happiness. The accuser's provocative question, "Does Job fear God for nothing?" (1:9) seems to persuade God to grant the satan limited destructive powers. Shown to be no friend of righteous Job, the satan afflicts him time and again with devastating losses. But in spite of tremendous trials, Job perseveres.

The Hebrew term *satan* is translated in the Septuagint (the Greek Bible) as *diabolos* (literally, "one who throws across," that is, an obstacle), from which the term "devil" derives. The *Catechism*, quoting the Fourth Lateran Council (1215 AD), teaches that "the devil and the other demons were indeed created naturally good by God, but they became evil by their own doing" (paragraph 391). The *Catechism* also explains that the petition "deliver us from evil" in the Our Father—the most ancient prayer of the Christian faith, taught by Jesus himself—"refers to a person, Satan, the Evil One, the angel who opposes God" (paragraph 2851). The oldest form of the prayer is found in Matthew 6:9–13:

> "Pray then in this way: / Our Father in heaven, / hallowed be your name. / Your kingdom come. / Your will be done, / on earth as it is in heaven. / Give us this day our daily bread. / And forgive us our debts, / as we also have forgiven our debtors. / And do not bring us to the time of trial, / but rescue us from the evil one."

In harmony with biblical depictions of Satan, the esteemed French scholar René Girard (1923–2015) regarded Satan as an entity with significant influence in the world, as reported by a biographer: "In Girard's eyes, Satan is the sower of discord: he is the public prosecutor and the executioner, the accuser and the jury foreman, spreading disorder, violence, and hatred wherever he goes. Satan is the contagion that reduces a population of individuals with distinct traits into a hysterical mob."[18]

Pope Francis, in his apostolic exhortation *Gaudete et Exsultate* (2018), warns that "we should not think of the devil as a myth, a representation, a symbol, a figure of speech or an idea. This mistake would lead us to let down our guard, to grow careless and end up more vulnerable. The devil does not need to possess us. He poisons us with the venom of hatred, desolation, envy and vice" (paragraph 161). Since his election in 2013 Pope Francis has repeatedly attributed today's evils, including the sex abuse scandal in the Catholic Church, to the work of the devil, whom he names "the malign one" and "the great accuser." Bishop Robert Barron follows suit, calling the sex abuse crisis "a diabolic masterpiece," for which abusive priests bear their own responsibility for the abuse and seduction of minors and others under their authority.[19] The hurt and devastation caused by such wickedness can hardly be overemphasized.

A Brief Scriptural Understanding of the Devil

The devil himself, in fact, does not appear in the Hebrew Bible, but does surface in the New Testament, where he is mentioned 35 times. After being punished by God in the Garden of Eden, the serpent became quite simply a snake made to slither on its belly. The account certainly explains why many humans do not like snakes. However, this wily serpent's influence was most definitely evil, and as evil in the world intensified beyond measure, so too grew the biblical impression of the dark nature of the serpent, which became synonymous with Satan.

The serpent was not the only creature to symbolize evil in ancient Israel, however. Israel shared with its cultural neighbors a fearful respect for a sea monster known as Leviathan, which in time also became thought of as a dragon. Dragons were depicted as serpentine creatures. Leviathan is mentioned twice in Job (3:8 and 41:1) and twice in the Psalms (74:14 and 104:26).

Ultimately, the mysterious forces of evil in the world which plotted in a special way against God's people (particularly the nations of Israel and Judah) became represented in the prophet Isaiah by three images: "On that day the LORD with his cruel and great and strong sword will punish Leviathan the fleeing serpent, Leviathan the twisting serpent, and he will kill the dragon that is in the sea" (Isaiah 27:1). The serpent, Leviathan, and the dragon were viewed as a single evil entity at enmity with God and God's people. Isaiah promised that God would defeat this evil beast. In the New Testament, Peter, whom Satan had demanded to sift "like wheat" (Luke 22:31), warns believers to resist the devil, whom he describes as a ravenous beast "looking for someone to devour" (1 Peter 5:8).

The author of Revelation equated the dragon with the ancient serpent who is unveiled as the devil and Satan (12:9). That the serpent is also the sea monster Leviathan seems evident in Revelation 12:15, in which the serpent "poured water like a river" in an attempt to drown the woman who bore the child who had been taken up into heaven. Historically the woman was interpreted as Mary, and by contemporary exegetes as a symbol of the people of God. The child is clearly Christ.

Demons in Media

Today, graphic novels and vivid films portray demons sprouting from hell to torment the living, both good and bad. The ancient rite of exorcism is enjoying renewed interest in Hollywood, which has never outgrown its fascination with demons and demonic possession.

In this current age, when antiheroes predominate in many storylines, it is no surprise that one of the more popular superhero types is a demon who, ironically, opposes evil, despite his origins. One example is Hellboy, a demon summoned from hell to earth by the Nazis, who becomes a rebel bent on countering the evil forces that thought they could control him.

In the satirical novel *The Screwtape Letters*, C. S. Lewis imaginatively portrays individual temptation through the character Wormwood, an inexperienced tempter who is mentored by the chief demon Screwtape. The focus in these these popular, though unsettling letters is on the demon's role in seducing his human "Patient" to commit seemingly minor misdeeds, rather than on the cosmic powers of darkness visible in oppressive systems, enslavement of all types, and horrors like the Shoah (meaning "destruction" or "catastrophe"; the Hebrew term for the Holocaust) that have scarred modern times.[20]

In the climactic scene of *The Godfather* (1972)—the highest grossing film at that time—Michael Corleone, invited to be his nephew's godfather, is asked by the priest to renounce Satan and all his works, as part of the baptismal rite. Michael makes a mockery of his promises to do so, for in close proximity to his affirmation of faith in the living God he orders opponents to be murdered, thus sealing in blood his transition into the role of Don Corleone, the godfather of the mafia.

One year later, the wildly popular horror film *The Exorcist*, which focused on the possibility of driving out demons, caught the public's imagination. Capitalizing on its overwhelming success, Hollywood produced two sequels and a film series. In the original story, Regan, a twelve-year-old girl, starts to act strangely after playing with an Ouija board. She uses obscene language, manifests extraordinary strength, and experiences her bed shaking violently. Two priests eventually manage to exorcise the demon from her, at the cost of their own lives. The movie was based on a book that drew on the experience of two priests who performed an exorcism in the 1940s. In that account the real-life possession and exorcism were far less dramatic, though perhaps no less dangerous, than the popular retellings. A critic from the *New York Times* dismissed the film as "a chunk of elegant occultist claptrap"; another labeled it "nothing more than a religious porn film." Nevertheless, the viewing public turned up in great numbers. Was this due to a fascination with embodied evil?

The path to become an exorcist is described in fascinating detail by Matt Baglio in *The Rite: The Making of a Modern Exorcist* (2010),[21] which chronicles the training and practice of Fr. Gary Thomas from the Diocese of San Jose (California), who participated in more than 80 exorcisms.

A year after this book appeared, the movie *The Rite* hit the screens. Like *The Exorcist*, this film brings the viewer into a world that assumes Satan is alive and active among human beings. Both the book and the movie recognize that in some cases the afflicted person may be dealing more with a mental illness than with demonic possession.

In this chapter we have considered the manifestation of demons in the Bible and the reality of evil forces in today's world. In the next chapter we will take a close look at disarming the evil one.

For Reflection

- Is demonic evil a reality that we must contend with today? If so, what resources or tools do Christians have to dispel this evil? What do you consider the gravest evils we deal with today?

- Do you believe Satan exists? If so, do you see Satan as personified evil?

Chapter Four

Dethroning the Evil One

The activity of the devil in the world is a cause for some alarm and caution, but not for fear or despair. Satan can tempt us to sin and persuade us to turn a blind eye to the evil actions of others, but his influence is hardly absolute. Jesus triumphed over Satan and all things evil, including the permanence of death, in his own death and resurrection. In this chapter we will see how Jesus' power and authority as the Son of God—both while he lived on earth and through the apostles and the Church after his resurrection—overpower the devil and weaken his hold on humanity.

Temptation and Evil

The nature of evil has always been dark and mysterious. The focus of divine revelation in Scripture is on God and the redemption of creation from the clutches of evil. However, as God's efforts to redeem take root in human history, the mystery of evil seems to grow darker and more intense. This was never more evident than in the shocking attack that turned deadly on the U.S. Capital by a mob of rioters on January 6, 2021. Struck by the sound of shattered windows and the occupation of sacred halls, Representative

Jim McGovern commented: "It was like looking at evil."[22] It all began in the Garden of Eden when, according to the etiological (meaning "explaining the origins of things") account, the serpent persuaded Eve to eat of the forbidden fruit which she, in turn, gave to her husband to eat:

> Now the serpent was more crafty than any other wild animal that the LORD God had made. He said to the woman, "Did God say, 'You shall not eat from any tree in the garden'?" The woman said to the serpent, "We may eat of the fruit of the trees in the garden; but God said, 'You shall not eat of the fruit of the tree that is in the middle of the garden, nor shall you touch it, or you shall die.'" But the serpent said to the woman, "You will not die; for God knows that when you eat of it your eyes will be opened, and you will be like God, knowing good and evil." So when the woman saw that the tree was good for food, and that it was a delight to the eyes, and that the tree was to be desired to make one wise, she took of its fruit and ate; and she also gave some to her husband, who was with her, and he ate. (Genesis 3:1–6)

The serpent is portrayed as a cynical, crafty, walking and talking reptile, and in this telling is not connected with either the devil or Satan. This identification only occurs much later (see Wisdom 2:24; Revelation 12:9, 20:2).

Without elaboration and with no mention of his status as an angel, Satan is identified as the tempter who led David to attempt to count the people of Israel (1 Chronicles 21:1, written during the fourth century BC). David is punished by God for this action, which was contemptuous of God's promise to Abraham that his offspring would be numerous beyond number: "I will make your offspring like the dust of the earth; so that if one can count the dust of the earth, your offspring also can be counted" (Genesis 13:16).

In the Book of Wisdom the evil most closely associated with the devil (again not yet identified as Satan) is envy (2:24). This verse informs us that through the envy of the devil death entered the world and gained a grip on humanity. The writer seems to imply that the serpent in Eden was the devil and that the fatal core of envy was the temptation to become like God.

This same temptation appears to be at the heart of a confrontation between Jesus and the Jews who accuse him of having a demon and who even seek to kill him (John 8:37,48). They argue with Jesus about his claims to be the Son of God, while claiming that they themselves are God's children because they are descendants of Abraham. Jesus' response is harsh. He claims that their enmity toward him makes them children of the devil.

> You are from your father the devil, and you choose to do your father's desires. He was a murderer from the beginning and does not stand in the truth, because there is no truth in him. When he lies, he speaks according to his own nature, for he is a liar and the father of lies. (John 8:44)

Identifying the devil as "a liar and the father of lies," the writer recalls the moment in the Garden of Eden when the serpent claimed that Eve would not die if she ate the fruit from the forbidden tree. The harsh language in this verse signals the ferocity in the conflict between the Jewish Christians in John's community and the synagogue authorities at the time.

Tragically, this verse has been taken out of context and used for anti-Semitic purposes. Such was the case with the murderer who gunned down 11 Jews at the Tree of Life Synagogue in Pittsburgh, PA, on October 27, 2018. This was the deadliest attack ever on Jews in the U.S. Branding Jews as the children of Satan, the shooter yelled "All Jews must die." Afterward, many religious leaders publicly condemned such hateful acts of bigotry and offered prayers in solidarity with the Jewish community.

Cast as a tempter, the devil makes his appearance in the Synoptic Gospels, which provide us with an account of Satan tempting Jesus in the wilderness—believed to be the favorite haunt of demons—following his baptism by John the Baptist. Matthew's and Luke's depictions of Jesus' temptation are much more descriptive than Mark's. In both Matthew and Luke, the devil claims the power to hand authority over the kingdoms of the earth to Jesus if only he will worship the tempter.

> The devil led him up and showed him in an instant all the kingdoms of the world. And the devil said to him, "To you I will give their glory and all this authority; for it has been given over to me, and I give it to anyone I please. If you, then, will worship me, it will all be yours." Jesus

answered him, "It is written, / 'Worship the Lord
your God, / and serve only him.'" (Luke 4:5–8)

Is this simply one of the lies of the devil? Do all the
kingdoms of the earth belong to Satan? This passage reflects
the Jewish people's experience of being subjected to various
world powers following the loss of their own kingdom and
of their line of rulers descended from David.

Throughout their history, the Jews, both those living
in Israel and in the diaspora ("scattering," referring to the
Jews forced out of Israel at different periods), are pain-
fully aware that the promises of God to grant Abraham's
offspring a land of their own have been crushed time and
again under the hooves and swords of foreign armies.
Joshua and the judges of Israel, through the invincible
power of God as their commander, had made Canaan
Israel's homeland, which was to be theirs in perpetuity.
Once, David had been assured of an everlasting dynasty
(2 Samuel 7:16), and Solomon had erected a temple of
unrivaled beauty to be the unique home of the Almighty
on earth. The importance of this unique dwelling place is
well attested in the Psalms.

> "Let us go to his dwelling place; / let us worship at
> his footstool." / Rise up, O LORD, and go to your
> resting place, / you and the ark of your might. . . .
> / For the LORD has chosen Zion; / he has desired
> it for his habitation: / "This is my resting place
> forever; / here I will reside, for I have desired it."
> (Psalm 132:7–8,13–14)

But the kings of Judah (David's progeny) rejected God's rule by turning to the idols of Israel's neighbors. The biblical record contains vivid accounts of God's punishment for doing so. The people of the promise to Abraham experienced exile, slavery, and domination by a series of kingdoms and empires throughout the course of nearly six centuries following the Babylonian invasion. At one time the Hellenistic Seleucid empire that grew out of the eastern portion of Alexander the Great's conquest attempted to eradicate Jewish religious practices completely.

In 63 BC, Palestine had become a vassal to the Roman Empire. By then, so prevalent was the belief that God had surrendered his authority over the kingdoms of the world that the person of Satan seemed to govern the nations of the earth. Satan's power would not be broken except by Jesus' own authority as the Son of God.

After the temptation in Luke's Gospel, the testing of Jesus reaches a critical point later in the narrative when his opponents accuse him of colluding with Beelzebul (or Beelzebub)—originally the title of the Canaanite fertility god Baal—described by Luke as "the ruler of the demons" (11:14–23). Jesus asserts that contrary to their slanderous accusation, he is stronger than Satan, for he casts out demons "by the finger of God" and thus brings about the kingdom of God in their midst. In the battle between the two kingdoms, God's and Satan's, it is the latter that falls. In the Book of Revelation an angel seals the fate of Satan: "He seized the dragon, that ancient serpent, who is the Devil and Satan, and bound him for a thousand years" (Revelation 20:2).

Jesus' Authority Over Demons

Jesus' authority over demons is extremely important in forming a better understanding of Jesus' mission to the people of Israel, and ultimately of his disciples' mission to the world at large. His authority not only testifies to the dignity and character of his identity as the Son of God (see e.g., Mark 1:24); it also demonstrates that Jesus came to bring healing to those afflicted with demons.

Jesus' activity of expelling demons is particularly prominent in Luke's Gospel, which highlights Jesus' ministry as one of combat with the evil powers that afflict the world. By exorcising demons, Jesus makes the kingdom of God a reality on earth ("has come near," see 9:27, 10:11). His stated purpose is to proclaim the good news of the kingdom (4:43). Luke clearly explains at the beginning of Jesus' public ministry what this good news means:

> When he came to Nazareth, where he had been brought up, he went to the synagogue on the sabbath day, as was his custom. He stood up to read, and the scroll of the prophet Isaiah was given to him. He unrolled the scroll and found the place where it was written:
>
> "The Spirit of the Lord is upon me,
> because he has anointed me
> to bring good news to the poor.
> He has sent me to proclaim release to the captives
> and recovery of sight to the blind,
> to let the oppressed go free,
> to proclaim the year of the Lord's favor."

. . . Then he began to say to them, "Today this scripture has been fulfilled in your hearing." (Luke 4:16–19,21)

Jesus truly sets captives and the oppressed free. They are the ones held in bondage by demons (unclean spirits), and his freeing of these victims is an endeavor closely aligned with healings such as recovery of sight for the blind. Just as the blind are healed, so also those held captive to demons are said to be cured when they are freed of the force that prevented them from living fully. Luke presents us with a world in the deep throes of oppression by evil spiritual forces. These demons are aligned with Satan, the head demon. Jesus commissions his disciples to continue his own ministry by going out into the towns of Israel: "Cure the sick who are there, and say to them, 'The kingdom of God has come near to you'" (Luke 10:9). When the disciples return to him they rejoice, exclaiming, "Lord, in your name even the demons submit to us!" Jesus affirms what they have experienced: "I watched Satan fall from heaven like a flash of lightning" (10:17–18). Jesus' mission as well as that of his disciples is to overthrow the demons, the evil forces of oppression in the world.

Luke briefly presents the case of Mary Magdalene, described as once having "seven demons" (8:2). The text does not address how these were manifested or how she was delivered from them.

A compelling account of Jesus' power over evil forces is that of his encounter with a person in the Gerasene region who was plagued with a multitude of demons (Luke 8:26–36). When Jesus and his disciples enter the region, they are met by "a man of the city who had demons." Luke explains that the man wore no clothes and lived in tombs outside the city. The demons immediately recognize Jesus and what he can do to them:

> When [the man] saw Jesus, he fell down before him and shouted at the top of his voice, "What have you to do with me, Jesus, Son of the Most High God? I beg you, do not torment me"— for Jesus had commanded the unclean spirit to come out of the man. (For many times it had seized him; he was kept under guard and bound with chains and shackles, but he would break the bonds and be driven by the demon into the wilds.) Jesus then asked him, "What is your name?" He said, "Legion"; for many demons had entered him. They begged him not to order them to go back into the abyss. (8:28-31)

The demons ask Jesus to let them enter a nearby herd of swine; when he gives them permission, they possess the swine and run them over a cliff into the sea. When the people come to see what happened, they find "the man from whom the demons had gone sitting at the feet of Jesus, clothed and in his right mind. And they were afraid" (8:35).

When Jesus asked the possessed person to name his demon, he replied with a number, "legion," not a name. In the Roman army, military units were divided into legions, each having between four and six thousand soldiers. This number underscores hyperbolically the magnitude of demonic forces that afflicted this unfortunate individual. That Luke is also making a political statement against the occupying power of Rome cannot be ruled out.

The Gerasene demoniac whom Jesus healed is homeless. Today, instead of being afflicted with demonic possession, many of the homeless are suffering from mental illnesses or addictions. Counselors and healthcare providers have several approaches and options to treat mental illnesses; exorcism is by no means to be considered a first line of intervention. In Luke's account, the man is bound in chains and shackles. Our homeless population endures one of the highest incarceration rates of any demographic. In Scripture, the demons, not their human victims, are meant to be bound! In healing the Gerasene, Jesus not only freed him from his demons, but he also apparently clothed him and liberated him from his shackles and chains, though we are not told how (see 8:35). One alarming aspect of this narrative is what happened to the demons. They entered the swine, and the herd rushed over a steep bank and drowned in a lake, implying they returned to an abyss.

Note that when the man is observed by his fellow citizens to be fully clothed and healed, he is also found to be sitting at the feet of Jesus. Such is the posture of a disciple receiving instruction. This encounter with Jesus might be an instruction to modern disciples on confronting diabolical evil in our midst.

Some of the illnesses Jesus cured through exorcism bear a strong resemblance to currently known medical conditions, and thus would not be considered a result of demonic possession today. This is the case with a possession Luke describes in 9:38–42 that appears to be a case of epilepsy.

> A man from the crowd shouted, "Teacher, I beg you to look at my son; he is my only child. Suddenly a spirit seizes him, and all at once he shrieks. It convulses him until he foams at the mouth; it mauls him and will scarcely leave him. I begged your disciples to cast it out, but they could not." Jesus answered, "You faithless and perverse generation, how much longer must I be with you and bear with you? Bring your son here." While he was coming, the demon dashed him to the ground in convulsions. But Jesus rebuked the unclean spirit, healed the boy, and gave him back to his father.

The restoration of relationships between children and parents is one of the signs of the end times ("the great and terrible day of the LORD") according to the prophet Malachi (4:5–6 [3:23–24 in some translations]).

We live in an age that has benefitted greatly from increases in scientific and medical knowledge. Modern medicine would scoff at the ancient biblical tendency to identify certain illnesses with demonic possession. Before rejecting Gospel accounts of demonic possession as merely scientific ignorance, however, a closer examination of the context in which Jesus performs his exorcism is warranted. Three points are helpful:

1) Jesus' exorcisms expel demons and result in healings for the afflicted victims. Hence the exorcisms are appropriately called a healing: "But Jesus rebuked the unclean spirit, healed the boy, and gave him back to his father" (Luke 9:42).

2) Jesus acted within a cultural context in which demonic possession was the most common understanding of certain conditions. Even the victims would have understood themselves as being possessed. The way in which Jesus is reported to have healed them was very important and relevant within the culture.

3) Jesus' healings of the demon-possessed are acts that restore individuals harmed by forces that impede their ability to function as whole human beings. For those who are attuned to the reality of evil, it should be easy, even today to recognize that such oppressive forces are the substance of evil. When Jesus heals the possessed, he does more than heal them as individuals; he also restores them to their communities and families.

Even those who doubt the reality of demons experience some unpleasantness, if not fear, in contemplating the idea of personal agents of evil. The biblical accounts of demons strongly suggest that they were (are), in fact, spiritual beings, probably angels, who are in league with Satan, the ultimate fallen angel, and are enemies of the human race. The demons Jesus encountered were frustrating the human potential of their victims. In healing demoniacs, Jesus empowered them to live fully human lives.

Exorcism of Demons

The practice of exorcism continued in the early church. In the Acts of the Apostles "some itinerant Jewish exorcists" failed to drive out evil spirits (19:13–16; see Luke 11:19), but Paul succeeded (Acts 16:16–18). When a slave-girl who had a spirit of divination followed him, the Apostle used the name of Jesus Christ to expel her annoying demon: "I order you in the name of Jesus Christ to come out of her." And so it did.

While the existence of demons as individual spiritual beings has been doubted by some Christian faithful in modern times, the disturbing reality of evil forces, inimical to human dignity is hard to overlook. To drive out these menacing, often destructive forces, the Church has the resource of exorcism, as stipulated in the *Catechism*: "When the Church asks publicly and authoritatively in the name of Jesus Christ that a person or object be protected against the power of the Evil One and withdrawn from his dominion, it is called *exorcism*" (paragraph 1673). The *Catechism* goes on to explain:

> In a simple form, exorcism is performed at the celebration of Baptism. The solemn exorcism,

called "a major exorcism," can be performed only by a priest and with the permission of the bishop. The priest must proceed with prudence, strictly observing the rules established by the Church. Exorcism is directed at the expulsion of demons or to the liberation from demonic possession through the spiritual authority which Jesus entrusted to his Church. Illness, especially psychological illness, is a very different matter; treating this is the concern of medical science. Therefore, before an exorcism is performed, it is important to ascertain that one is dealing with the presence of the Evil One, and not an illness. (1673)

In the Rite of Baptism, the baptismal candidate is asked to take a definitive stance against the lure of evil: "Do you reject Satan? And all his works? And all his empty promises?" A definitive "I do" is expected in response to each of these inquiries. The practice of renouncing Satan can be traced back to the early days of the Church. Tertullian attested that before baptism is received "we solemnly swear that we disown the devil and his pomp and his angels." Jesus had firsthand experience with Satan's empty promises during his sojourn in the desert. In dangling before Jesus the temptation to the exercise of unbridled power (Matthew 4:8-9, Luke 4:6-7), the devil offered what he could not provide. For, as the risen Jesus attests at the end of Matthew's Gospel: "All authority in heaven and on earth has been given to me" (28:18).

Following the repudiation of Satan, his works, and his promises, baptismal candidates are called upon to affirm their faith in God, the Father Almighty; in Jesus Christ; and in the Holy Spirit. Succumbing to the allure of Satan is incompatible with belief in the living God, a Trinity of Persons, the very foundation of the deposit of faith. Baptismal promises are renewed by candidates at Confirmation and by all the faithful in the Easter Vigil. At Confirmation, the candidates are asked once again to denounce Satan and to reaffirm their belief in the Father, Son, and Holy Spirit. Then the bishop solemnly declares: "This is our faith. This is the faith of the Church. We are proud to profess it in Christ Jesus our Lord."

To conduct exorcisms of those possessed by demons, bishops of many Roman Catholic dioceses appoint a specially trained priest to serve as an exorcist. The spike in interest is described by Fr. Vincent Lampert, the exorcist for the Archdiocese of Indianapolis, who reported having received 1,900 inquiries regarding evil spirits in 2018. He received his formal training for this role at the Pontifical North American College in Rome.

Stories of recent exorcism cases are not hard to find in the news. In a case in 2008, a group of doctors from New York Medical College concurred that a woman who levitated six inches off the ground and manifested paranormal powers was possessed by a devil. A nine-year-old boy in Gary, Indiana, was observed in 2012 doing strange things like walking up the side of a wall. In his case the exorcist was Fr. Michael Maginot, pastor of St. Stephen, Martyr Church in nearby Merrillville, Indiana.

The demand for trained exorcists is so great that the Vatican is hardly able to recruit enough of them; it is not a task to be undertaken lightly. One Catholic online news source proclaims that the world is under attack—an "army of demons has led to a spike in exorcisms."[23] Fr. Lampert believes that the rising tide of drug use, the occult, and pornography serves as an entry point for evil. Many walk through that door and seem to be under the influence of the demonic. We should never underestimate the attraction that evil has for many people nor its ability to hold sway in their lives once they let it in.

Jesus Conquers Evil

John's Gospel and Paul's letters and preaching acknowledge that the devil once ruled the world and its kingdoms. However, through his death and resurrection, Jesus became king of all (John) and Lord of all (Paul, e.g. Acts 10:36). In the Fourth Gospel Jesus announces: "Now is the judgment of this world; now the ruler of this world will be driven out. And I, when I am lifted up from the earth, will draw all people to myself" (John 12:31–32). For Paul the domination of evil forces on earth is ubiquitous, reigning even from above: "For our struggle is not against enemies of blood and flesh, but against the rulers, against the authorities, against the cosmic powers of this present darkness, against the spiritual forces of evil in the heavenly places" (Ephesians 6:12).

Jesus, through his resurrection from the dead, ultimately conquered Satan and dethroned him by stripping him of his greatest power, the power of death. In First Corinthians we are told that Jesus' death and resurrection revealed the secret wisdom and plan of God to strip power from the evil dominions of the earth:

> We speak God's wisdom, secret and hidden, which God decreed before the ages for our glory. None of the rulers of this age understood this; for if they had, they would not have crucified the Lord of glory. (2:7–8)

In chapter 15 Paul proclaims that in the end the victorious Christ will destroy "every ruler and every authority and power." Neither the Roman imperial rulers of that age nor the demonic forces of evil that have afflicted humankind from the beginning will survive, for all things will be subjected to the rule of God (15:24–28).

Whatever power the devil—taken seriously as the embodiment of evil and not some miniature crimson cartoon character with a pitchfork—may still possess in the world, through the power of God in Christ he has been dethroned as its emperor. The kingdoms of the earth do not belong to him. Jesus is the Lord of glory (1 Corinthians 2:8). Evil still exists, and the devil still roams about, seeking whom he might harm ("Like a roaring lion your adversary the devil prowls around, looking for someone to devour" [1 Peter 5:8]), but he can be resisted, because those who serve Christ serve the one who was completed victorious over all evil. In the next chapter we will explore the world of superheroes, ancient and contemporary, as well as themes from the Book of Revelation, which underscore God's ultimate victory of good over evil through the centrality of Jesus' death and resurrection.

For Reflection

- In what ways are you called to resist the forces of evil in your community?

- What insights does the awareness that Jesus' exorcisms are also called healings offer as you ponder demonic possessions as portrayed in the Gospels?

Chapter Five

Heroes and Villains and Worlds Beyond

Today it seems that there are more superheroes than there are superpowers for them to wield. What stirs the modern imagination to create so many superheroes? They are really nothing new. After all, Greek and Roman mythology filled the heavens and the earth with gods, who created and protected nearly every aspect of human life, and their human offspring, the demi-gods. For fire there was the god Hephaestus (or Vulcan, to the Romans), and for the mighty ocean waves and horses with their stampeding power and wave-like manes, there was Poseidon (or Neptune).

Superheroes in the Christian Worldview

The biblical world also had its superheroes. Three celestial heroes who stand out are the archangels and great princes Michael, Gabriel, and Raphael, whom we encountered earlier. They are acclaimed for their respective roles as protector, messenger, and rescuer. Michael is a great warrior who defeated Satan (Revelation 12:7–8) and is believed to have had a central role in ending the devastating plague that raged in Rome in 590—his statue above Castel Sant'Angelo recalls that event. In a homily on the feast of

Michael the Archangel, Gregory the Great (who was pope from 590–604) said, "Whenever something is to be done needing great power, Michael is sent forth so that from his action and his name we may understand that no one can do what God can do." The artist Raphael captures this superhero well, showing him clad in armor and carrying spear and sword in his painting "St. Michael Vanquishing Satan" (created in 1518). Along with Michael, the other two superheroes—Gabriel, known as the powerful messenger of God, and Raphael, known as the power who drives away a demon—appear regularly throughout the Bible.

Living in biblical times when these and other heavenly beings made their appearance must have seemed like living in a magical, enraptured universe. However, this world was not only enchanted by these beneficent spiritual heroes; it was also afflicted by the menacing presence of the devil and his minions, as we saw. This was certainly true in the first century when many longed for a Judea free from all foreign domination by the Romans, whose rule was experienced as demonic. The devil had taken charge of history, and it took a powerful act of divine intervention, in the person of God's Messiah, to free the people of Judea and to bestow upon them the many divine promises made to their ancestors. As Christians embraced faith in Jesus of Nazareth, the risen Christ—which literally means "God's anointed"—they began to view the world in a new way. To be sure, the devil still had influence, but he had been decisively defeated and any power he had on earth came to an ominous end with the thrashing of a dying beast, as described in the Book of Revelation: "[W]oe to the earth and the sea, / for the devil has come down to you / with great wrath, / because he knows that his time is short!" (12:12, see 19:11-21).

With the coming of Jesus, a kingdom with power much greater—and of a different nature—than Rome's became available to his followers. Jesus began his ministry by announcing that the kingdom of God was already making its appearance: "Now after John was arrested, Jesus came to Galilee, proclaiming the good news of God, and saying, 'The time is fulfilled, and the kingdom of God has come near; repent, and believe in the good news'" (Mark 1:14–15). These two verses summarize well Jesus' entire proclamation. The decisive moment appointed by God is being realized in the words and deeds of this Galilean peasant.

The Christian worldview that eventually predominated in Europe was one in which spiritual powers, in the form of angels, and increasingly that of saints as well, played a dynamic role in the lives of believers. There were evil spiritual powers, to be sure, but good angels and the prayers of saints were always available to the faithful for daily protection in their struggle against evil. The world itself, having been created by a loving God, was a gift which, when properly appreciated, helped bring human creatures into a spiritual communion with the Creator. Everything that had being was a sign and a reminder to the person of faith of the One who created it. Some philosophers would call this perception of reality a belief in an enchanted world. Ludwig Wittgenstein (1889–1951), for example, described his experience as "seeing the world as a miracle." God's creation filled him with astonishment that prompted him to say, "how extraordinary that the world should exist."[24]

Following the European enlightenment of the eighteenth century, however, philosophers increasingly began to accept a purely materialistic definition of reality, rejecting any need for a creator at all (atheism), or at least denying any interaction between the world and its far distant Creator (deism). The spiritual aura that monotheism found in creation simply vanished from their view. This disappearance is often referred to as the disenchantment of the world (or universe).

Though many do claim we now live in a disenchanted world, there is evidence that our culture yearns for a return to enchantment. The Christian perspective of a material world that only thinly veils a world filled with God's presence has never ceased to have a strong, creative voice. Perhaps the modern imagination has created for us an attempt to return, at least in fantasy, to those seemingly magical, enchanted times.

A Poetic and Literary Point of View

Gerard Manley Hopkins (1844–1889), an English poet and Jesuit, was already sensitive to the befogging of creation's enchantment by the steam engines of the industrial revolution. In his timeless poem "God's Grandeur," he beautifully affirms the divinely enchanted nature of creation while lamenting how thoroughly human endeavors can blind us to it.

The world is charged with the grandeur of God.
  It will flame out, like shining from shook foil;
  It gathers to a greatness, like the ooze of oil
Crushed. Why do men then now not reck his rod?

  . . .

And for all this, nature is never spent;
  There lives the dearest freshness deep down
  things.[25]

To this poet the grandeur of God is indeed charged with a mysterious, vibrant luster when seen through the eyes of faith. With or without any explicit faith, popular culture has never been comfortable with a disenchanted universe. The contemporary appetite for what can be called the "supernatural" only grows as the claims of materialistic perspectives abound. Whether this is poetic irony or a backlash against modernism, the imagination of those from East to West is still preoccupied with the godlike powers of supernatural beings.

This disenchantment of the enlightenment means that we have, culturally, largely lost our awareness of personal beings wielding and acting on behalf of the forces of good and evil. But humanity is still deeply conscious that good and evil exist and are actively opposed to each other.

Regarding the latter, Cardinal Gregory of Washington D.C. forcefully stated: "We have lots of evil spirits that somehow are destroying the harmony of the nation, making people of different races and cultures and languages and religions afraid of one another" (January 2021).[26]

Millions of spectators spend billions of dollars to have their senses jolted by any sort of encounter with imaginary beings and their incredible powers. These beings enthrall moviegoers, titillate readers, and play with us in toys and games. Fans crowd together in the thousands, many of them donning the masks and uniforms of their superheroes in what is called "cosplay" (costumed role playing), to meet the famous actors who have brought their fantasies to life. (In 2019 over 180,000 people attended Comic Con in San Diego and about three quarters of a million participated in a similar event in Tokyo.) Whether real or imaginary, supernatural beings—and the forces of good and evil they represent—populate our cosmos in any form they can.

Judeo-Christian culture has had a profound influence on popular depictions of good and evil and the beings who fight for them. One of the earliest and most popular superheroes, Superman, was imbued with messianic characteristics by his Jewish creators, Jerry Siegel and Joe Shuster. Superman's origins also have strong parallels with the Exodus account of Moses (2:1–3). Both Moses and Superman were "shipped off" as infants from their own people to be raised elsewhere, safe from harm. In adulthood, both became heroic figures with supernatural powers used to protect those oppressed by evil forces.

Notable also are the Christian writers who themselves have had tremendous impact in fashioning fantasy worlds; their works invite appreciation for spiritual realities, including specifically Christian ones, alive in the real world. This is particularly true of *The Space Trilogy* and the *Chronicles of Narnia* by C. S. Lewis and *The Lord of the Rings* and other works of Middle Earth by his friend J. R. R. Tolkien.

As we have seen above in Chapter Two, *The Space Trilogy* features *eldila*, extraterrestrial, holy, and immortal beings who inhabit "deep space." Functioning like angels, they accomplish the work of the Almighty. On earth there are "dark eldila," fallen angels or demons. Throughout his writings Lewis portrays angels as real beings who are part of God's providence, participating in the lives of humans.

The *Chronicles*, often treated as an allegory, are stories meant to illuminate what is truly important about our own world. The hero is the lion Aslan, whose role closely resembles that of Jesus Christ, identified in Revelation 5:5 as "the Lion of the tribe of Judah." For Lewis the connection between his faith and fantasy was explicit; for Tolkien it was more implicit. Yet Tolkien insisted that he did not create the worlds he wrote about, for there is only one Creator—God—and that he and other artists are simply makers who play with what God has already created.[27]

Both Tolkien and Lewis fashioned their imaginary worlds as realms where definitive struggles between good and evil took place. But while Lewis made an allegorical Christ figure the center of his Narnia, Tolkien let his humble, frail, and error-prone hobbits stumble into victory over evil through the invisible guidance of Providence. It is the meekness of these diminutive creatures that allows them to build and inhabit a peaceful world when the proud and the powerful forces of evil could not.

Tolkien reinvented the fantasy genre, but today perhaps no fictional realm enjoys the success of J. K. Rowling's *Harry Potter* series. Good and evil witches and wizards match wits and cast spells as Harry and his friends struggle with all the typical issues of children maturing into young adults. While there is little ostensibly Christian about this series, it is set against a backdrop of enduring Christian culture, where even Hogwarts' students and professors acknowledge Christmas (albeit without Christ) as an important holiday. Some Christian leaders have warned that the fascination with magic, witches, and wizards is inimical to Christianity. Yet most Christian fans of Harry Potter, who number in the millions, insist that what is most Christian about the series is also what is most central to it: its awareness of good and evil and the importance of fighting for goodness whatever the personal cost.

Heroes and villains in media have become more human, like the gods of myth, and unlike angels and demons, who are a different kind of creation and inhabit a different level of existence, so to speak. However, it is typical of modern supervillains to claim godlike superiority over humans and therefore the right to rule them, with a vanity that is perhaps reminiscent of Satan's confidence that the world is his to give. Like the ancient pantheons of gods, modern superheroes regularly exhibit the same moral shortcomings of human nature despite any godlike powers they might possess. Few of today's superheroes present the bashful humility and shy but polite demeanor of the earliest portrayals of Superman's alter ego, Clark Kent. Instead they often act on the darker sides of human nature, even as they protect humanity from evil forces within and without the human race. Those familiar with Hellboy, Deadpool,

Wolverine, and other prominent super "heroes" know that there is a thin line that separates a superhero from a supervillain. Does the growing popularity of heroes who struggle with whether and how to "do good" reflect the fears and turmoil of modern life?

Indeed, it seems that what superheroes provide modern audiences most is an answer to our ever-burgeoning need to escape mundane—and unjust—reality. Their stories offer the reassurance that when existence as we know it does begin to crumble—or explode—we will know what to do, and that out of the ensuing chaos good will prevail. Fictional wars between good and evil increasingly place the threat of misused technology at the heart of futuristic struggles, for instance. Artificial intelligence runs amok in plot after plot. Also, pandemics like COVID-19, the threat of climate change, and other ecological disasters leave only the heroes and what remains of humanity to fight for survival in a struggling world.

Ancient tales of angelic warfare from biblical times are frequently used as springboards for modern apocalyptic machinations. The dark comedy series *Good Omens*, reminiscent of the 1999 spoof *Dogma*, makes satirical use of scriptural themes in every segment. The 2009 movie *Watchmen* employed a menagerie of superheroes in roles reminiscent of the good and evil angels known as the "watchers" in Daniel and the apocryphal books of Enoch.

In Daniel 4:17, the "watchers" are angels who oversee and pass sentence from the Most High on the affairs of human beings. Through them God maintains his sovereignty over the world. In the books of Enoch, the watchers include many fallen angels, among whom, as we have seen, are those referred to in Genesis 6:1–4 as the "sons of God" who came down to earth to mate with human women. In Revelation, the martyrs invoke God's sovereignty in a plea for judgment and vindication, in a vision reminiscent of Daniel's description.

> I saw under the altar the souls of those who had been slaughtered for the word of God and for the testimony they had given; they cried out with a loud voice, "Sovereign Lord, holy and true, how long will it be before you judge and avenge our blood on the inhabitants of the earth?" (Revelation 6:9–10)

The End of the World as We Know It

Angels play a significant role in biblical descriptions of the end times—sometimes called "the last things"—and other end-times writings from that era, similar to that of superheroes in contemporary fictional end-of-the-world scenarios (commonly called apocalypses, after the Greek name for the Book of Revelation, where many of these descriptions are found). Doomsday fears have haunted humanity throughout the centuries, but there is a key difference between how Scripture depicts the final confrontation between good and evil and how modern fantasies wage their seemingly endless battles with ultimate evil.

Perhaps the battles between good and evil in modern fantasies attempt to inspire trust that goodness will prevail in the end. By contrast, the consistent message of biblical apocalypses is one of hope for real people confronted with real evil. They are addressed to marginalized believers, who struggled to maintain their identity as a people especially beloved by God when the forces of history and worldly power conspired to destroy them.

Scripture reflects a real conflict between good and evil, one we can witness ourselves, in a struggle that involves both heaven and earth—a conflict that, moreover, has already been won by the Son of God, as we have seen. The battle of good angels against wicked angels is real. There is a pressing need for courage and hope in trying times, and the help offered by the angels and saints of the victorious God serves as a valuable resource. Such assistance provides hope and confidence. On the other hand, the half-Atlantean/half-human superhero Aquaman, for example, may appeal to the imagination but does not offer hope to a real family worried about a sailor at sea.

The angels, as described in the Letter to the Hebrews, are powerful agents of God whose purpose is to assist our ultimate well-being: "Are not all angels spirits in the divine service, sent to serve for the sake of those who are to inherit salvation?" (1:14). As we saw in Jesus' parables in the Gospel of Matthew, the angels will stand as witnesses when the righteous inherit salvation. We will see in the following chapters some of the ways angels are "sent to serve" for our sake.

What is lost if a biblical worldview is traded for a science fiction or fantasy lens? Scripture has the power to fire the human imagination, while also allowing us to locate ourselves firmly within this imponderable world given to us by our Creator. When our life is imbued with a biblical perspective, we dwell as beings both magnificent and humble; magnificent because, in the language of Psalm 8, we have been created "a little lower than God, / and crowned . . . with glory and honor" (verse 5). The Hebrew term rendered "God" (NRSV, compare to "a god" in NABRE) is *elohim*, also translated "heavenly beings" (NET) or "angels" (NKJV; and see Hebrews 2:7). While we have been given divine-like powers to do good, we maintain a humble stance because we remain creatures who require faith to make our way through this world. With that in mind, we are called, in the spirit of Psalm 8, to praise our Creator who has exalted the human creature.

O Lord, our Sovereign,
    how majestic is your name in all the earth!
You have set your glory above the heavens.
    Out of the mouths of babes and infants
you have founded a bulwark because of your foes,
    to silence the enemy and the avenger.
When I look at your heavens, the work of your fingers,
    the moon and the stars that you have established;
what are human beings that you are mindful of them,
    mortals that you care for them?
Yet you have made them a little lower than God,
    and crowned them with glory and honor.
You have given them dominion over the works
    of your hands;

> you have put all things under their feet,
> all sheep and oxen,
> > and also the beasts of the field,
> the birds of the air, and the fish of the sea,
> > whatever passes along the paths of the seas.
> O Lord, our Sovereign,
> > how majestic is your name in all the earth!

There seems to be little benefit in trading faith for fantasy, however enticing this may be. Faith itself stokes our imagination and our will with the freedom to go beyond our limited senses. Faith opens the mind and the heart to explore the universe and beyond! Armed with an ancient faith and a hungry imagination, perhaps we might see in ourselves a deeply ingrained need for a world "charged with the grandeur of God," a reality beyond our grasp. Otherwise, as the poet Robert Browning so aptly queries, "what's a heaven for?"[28] One dimension of the reality beyond our normal perception, yet prominent in popular spirituality, is the realm of guardian angels, to which we now turn.

For Reflection

- What superheroes in the Christian realm, whether angels or saints, inspire you and fire your imagination?

- What superheroes in the secular world have attracted your attention? How do they relate to your life of faith?

Chapter Six

Guardian Angels and Angels of Doom

As a boy attending St. Michael's School in Brookville, Indiana, I was among the countless numbers of Catholic children who were taught this prayer to our guardian angels:

> Angel of God, my guardian dear, to whom God's love commits me here, ever this day (or night) be at my side, to light and guard, to rule and guide. Amen.

I recall being given a holy card with an adult-sized angel standing close behind a young child. By regularly saying this prayer—inspired by the Benedictine monk Reginald of Canterbury (c. 1040–1109)—I felt a sense of safety day and night provided by my personal angel, over and above the security I felt growing up cared for by my parents, teachers, and the local community. Though not forgotten, that daily devotion has been enriched by an underlying belief in God's providential care, even when I have gone astray.

Angels Standing Guard

In a memorable and moving scene in the opera *Hansel and Gretel* (first performed in 1893), the children, who are alone and lost in the woods, sing "Evening Prayer," also known as "The Children's Prayer." It begins: "When at night I go to sleep, / Fourteen angels watch do keep." The lyrics continue by naming seven sets of two angels who stand at their head, feet, right hand, and left hand, and "warmly cover," hover over, and guide their "steps to heaven." Immediately after the song, fourteen angels take the stage and gather around the children to protect them and keep them safe. Then the forest fills with light. In real life, angels do protect us; and they also, in the words of Pope St. John XXIII, intercede for the believer: "I am ever under the gaze of an angel who protects and prays for me."

The belief in the role of angels implied in this and related traditions is clearly articulated in the *Catechism*, which professes that "from infancy to death human life is surrounded by [angels'] watchful care and intercession" (paragraph 336). Names of churches throughout the world, such as the Church of the Guardian Angel in Manhattan, honor the role of angels as guardians and protectors in the lives of the faithful.

The biblical tradition provides the foundation for our belief in the guiding and protecting role of angels. After Adam and Eve are expelled from the garden, angels in the form of cherubim (winged supernatural beings) are placed by the Lord God "to guard the way to the tree of life" (Genesis 3:24), which is the source of immortality. At first glance this may seem to be a harsh punishment, but at a closer look it is apparent that God's action saved human beings from becoming something other than what they were created to be. Having disobeyed God by eating from the tree of the knowledge of good and evil, how much mischief might humans have conjured up had they become immortal by eating from the tree of life? God guarded the tree of life so that human beings would not be eternally separated from the Divine in their state of sin.

Next we turn to the story of Lot, his wife, and their two daughters. Had the two angels not intervened and instructed Lot to get up and leave Sodom, his family would have been consumed in the punishment of the city (Genesis 19:15). A few chapters later, an angel appears on the scene just in time to prevent Abraham from taking the life of his own son, through whom God's promise would be carried out (Genesis 22:11–12). Some people today may look back on a close call—an almost inevitable tragic car accident avoided, a son who recovered from a debilitating addiction, a woman who escapes life-threatening abuse from a violent partner—and attribute it to the action of their guardian angel. I have a 30 year old nephew with severe disabilities. His devoted mother believes that he must have a thousand angels watching over him, pulling him through countless seizures and protecting him from harm.

The Christian belief in guardian angels—that each person has a specific angel watching over her or him—can be traced back at least to the third century. A feast of the guardian angels has been celebrated since the sixteenth century. The one New Testament text that clearly refers to guardian angels occurs in the Gospel of Matthew. Jesus says: "Take care that you do not despise one of these little ones; for, I tell you, in heaven their angels continually see the face of my Father in heaven" (Matthew 18:10). In verse 6 "these little ones" are identified as those "who believe in me," and thus refers to all disciples of Jesus, not specifically to children. These angels are assigned to believers and constantly behold the face of God. They do not have to physically travel back and forth between heaven and earth; they are well positioned to represent the needs and concerns of their charges to the Father.

There are also moments in the biblical account that can only be understood as miraculous, accomplished by divine intervention. How is it, for example, that the fleeing Israelites were able to escape the powerful pharaoh of Egypt and his numerous warriors? The narrator attributes this to angelic protection: "The angel of God who was going before the Israelite army moved and went behind them; and the pillar of cloud moved from in front of them and took its place behind them" (Exodus 14:19; see 23:20,23). This angel protected and guarded them on their way to the place God had prepared for them.

The psalmist declares that the Most High "will command his angels concerning you / to guard you in all your ways" (91:11), as they did during the devil's temptation of Jesus. The devil himself cited the next verse of this psalm: "On their hands they will bear you up, / so that you will not dash your foot against a stone" (Matthew 4:6, see Psalm 91:12); he tried to twist its meaning, however. The rhetorical question in the Letter to the Hebrews, "Are not all angels spirits in the divine service, sent to serve for the sake of those who are to inherit salvation?" (1:14), manifests the writer's conviction that angels are indeed at the service of the divine for the sake of human beings.

In addition to guardian angels, the Bible also describes angels of death. In one instance the Lord sends an angel to bring destruction to Jerusalem (2 Samuel 24:16); in another instance an angel annihilates an entire camp of the Assyrians, slaughtering 135,000 soldiers (2 Kings 19:35; see also 2 Maccabees 15:22). That the biblical writers would put such destruction on the moral ledger of angels, God's messengers, is astounding, and surely difficult to explain. Was the level of destruction so great, the only way they knew to explain it was divine causality? God often acts on behalf and in defense of his chosen people in the Old Testament, so perhaps angelic warriors are simply one of the ways God brings about their victory in his name. Jesus briefly refers to the angels' capacity as warriors when the chief priests send guards to arrest him. He stops his disciples from fighting the guards, saying, "Do you think that I cannot appeal to my Father, and he will at once send me more than twelve legions of angels?" (Matthew 26:53). The angels stood ready to defend the Son of God, if defense had indeed been called for in that moment.

Angels seem to work at preserving life in desperate circumstances, even surrounded by the horrors of death.

After his parents and six siblings had been taken from the Warsaw ghetto to the death camp in Treblinka, Shmuel was also rounded up by the Nazis and lined up against a wall to be executed by a firing squad. The fourteen-year-old child, through some mysterious visitation, heard his grandfather say "Don't give up! You will live!" At that same moment the commander told the gunman, "Take him out. He will die later." And so Shmuel was spared. After the war, he asked Miriam Greenspan, whose relatives were killed in Auschwitz and Treblinka but whose parents escaped, what she made of his story. She answered, "The angels must have been very busy during the Holocaust." Greenspan reflects that Shmuel's angel is "just one story of the sacred at work in the daily lives and events in the world."[29] Why some are rescued and others are not is a question beyond both the scope of this book and human understanding, though we are encouraged to ponder this in our dialogue with God.

The presence of angels can be a source of comfort. In a poignant text found only in the Gospel of Luke, the evangelist demonstrates this effect during Jesus' intense agony before his death: "Then an angel from heaven appeared to him and gave him strength. In his anguish he prayed more earnestly, and his sweat became like great drops of blood falling down on the ground" (22:43–44). Just as an angel brought strength to a suffering Jesus, so also God may extend sustaining help either directly or, as some patients experience, through an angel. In the *Ars Moriendi* (Art of Dying), a popular devotional in the fifteenth century for those on their death bed, an angel is pictured in two block print scenes at a bedside to assist the dying to maintain hope in the face of despair and to be patient, as was Jesus during his last hours.

When his own life was in danger aboard a ship violently pounded by waves, the apostle Paul was visited by an angel. Urging the crew to keep up their courage, Paul shared with them the angel's reassuring message: "For last night there stood by me an angel of the God to whom I belong and whom I worship, and he said, 'Do not be afraid, Paul; you must stand before the emperor; and indeed, God has granted safety to all those who are sailing with you'" (Acts 27:23–24).

On the Feast of Guardian Angels in 2018, Pope Francis reminded the faithful that guardian angels are the help "the Lord promises his people and us who walk along the path of life."[30] He added that as companions and protectors, guardian angels are like "a human compass or a compass that resembles a human being and helps us see where we should go" to avoid dangers and getting lost along the way. The pope continued with what to many would seem to be a surprising series of questions: "Do you speak to your angel? . . . Do you listen to your angel? Do you let yourself be taken by the hand along the path or [be] pushed to move?" He encouraged Christians to pray to their guardian angel who "is not only with us but also sees God" and is "the daily door toward transcendence, to the encounter" with the Divine. Such dialogue invites the faithful to foster an intimacy with our heavenly guides, enabling us to be more aware of their prompting and protection.

Angelic Encounters

In a well-documented 2001 study of 350 ordinary people who believed they had "encountered an angelic presence," Emma Heathcote-James reported that almost one-third claimed to have seen angels as they are understood traditionally. These angels were clearly spiritual beings: winged, radiant, translucent, and often dressed in white.[31] Others described "human" angels with superhuman qualities, dressed in contemporary clothes. The majority of those who reported experiences of angels were Christian; almost ten percent were either agnostic or atheist. Heathcote-James evaluated the respondents for psychological factors, possible hallucinations, and post-traumatic mechanisms. There remained remarkable occurrences that eluded rational explanations. It is instructive to cite one example.

A child was brought into the emergency room with just a scratch on his head after he was run over by a truck—both sets of wheels, according to eyewitnesses. When the child woke up he reported having seen a "man in the long shiny dress . . . he stroked my face, as he picked up the wheels . . . the wheels did not touch me."[32] The child did not say it was a guardian angel, or use the word "angel" at all. This experience seems too incredible to believe. Was this an "angel," or were other factors and forces involved? The case was reported by a medical student, a firm atheist. How this experience affected the student afterward is unknown.

Once a young college student in my Death, Dying and Afterlife class showed me a small statue of a white angel with gold wings that "has never left my side." Her mother gave it to her when she was fourteen. "I am a religious person," the student explained, "so I do believe that angels look over us, and I do believe that this angel looks over me especially since it came from my mom, and even more when I am not with my mom to looks over me." Sounds like a guardian angel at work! With guardian angels appearing in everything from country songs to bestselling books, it's clear that the idea of having an angel assigned to look out for us is appealing and comforting to many.

Sometimes ordinary beneficial circumstances are attributed to the intervention of a guardian angel. Ricky Manalo, CSP, a liturgical composer who teaches at Santa Clara University, relates a time when he traveled by air in January during two major storms and a polar vortex. Although thousands of flights were delayed and cancelled, miraculously all of Manalo's five flights departed on time. Afterward he thought, "I must have a guardian angel!" Whether or not he meant this statement literally, his reaction expresses a belief that the ups and downs of our daily lives do not go unnoticed by God.

Guardian Angels throughout History

The belief that heavenly beings protect, guide, and guard individual humans has a long history going back to the ancient Sumerian, Akkadian, and Babylonian cultures, which believed that lower deities were assigned to humans. The Greeks believed that when members of the first race died they became "pure spirits" who roamed over the earth and served as guardians for mortals. The biblical writers undoubtedly were aware of these associations from their cultural context, and hence it would have made sense to tell stories about the link between heaven and earth facilitated by divine messengers, who came to be called angels.

Even before the belief that individual angels are assigned to watch over individual human beings became prominent, angels were also designated as protectors of nations. The Deuteronomist remarks that "When the Most High apportioned the nations, / when he divided human-kind, / he fixed the boundaries of the peoples / according to the number of the gods" (Deuteronomy 32:8, translated in the Septuagint as "according to the angels of God"). Darrell Hannah concludes that this verse "affirmed a belief in heavenly guardians, whether lesser deities or angels, set over the nations as a kind of cosmic patron."[33]

In the Book of Exodus God assigns an angel to watch over the Hebrew people as they travel through the desert: "I am going to send an angel in front of you, to guard you on the way and to bring you to the place that I have prepared" (Exodus 23:20). In the Book of Daniel, the prophet assures Israel that they have Michael as their great prince, their celestial champion and protector (Daniel 10:13,21; 12:1). Through this celestial warrior, God assures an oppressed and persecuted people that they will emerge victorious. Joan of Arc (1412–1431) noted that the inspiration of Michael the Archangel helped her defeat the English during the Hundred Years' War. Less than a century later, in response to a plea from the Portuguese king, Julius II (pope from

1503–1513) established a feast for Michael as the Guardian Angel of Portugal. Also known as the Angel of Peace, Michael is said to have visited young Lucia, Francisco, and Jacinta at Fatima in 1916 to prepare them to carry out the work of the Blessed Virgin Mary.

In the Care of Angels

Recently, a talented pastoral care student who grew up in the Church of Jesus Christ of Latter Day Saints shared with me her own belief that she herself has several guardian angels and archangels. Once she described herself through a dramatic portrait of an angel, whose head, shoulders, and even wings were drooped down, weighted with the sorrow and despair of the world. Naming herself an "earth angel," this student sees herself as a source of light for others, reminding them that they are loved by God and have a purpose. Although the idea of functioning as an "earth angel" may be appealing, one would be hard put to find a biblical foundation for such a belief. We can remember, however, that heavenly angels are not the only beings who can bring the good news of God's love and peace to people on earth.

Indeed sometimes in common usage the line between guardian angels and humans becomes blurred. A large healthcare system in Southern California, for example, has established a way to recognize exceptional caregivers called the Guardian Angel Program. Recipients of care in this system are invited to honor their "guardian angel" by donating to the hospital foundation. Another example is the volunteer non-profit organization called Border Angels. They serve the immigrant population in several ways, by providing legal assistance, placing bottles of water along migrant crossing routes, and in general advocating for the rights of those fleeing for their lives from countries torn apart by violence. A third group, Hells Angels, has a checkered history. Known for riding in packs on loud Harleys, wearing leather jackets, and occasional run-ins with law enforcement, they also, on the positive side, raise money for charities, organize toy drives at Christmas, and regularly conduct food drives. Each of these groups appeals to our "better angels," a metaphor we will discuss below.

What about messages from angels? Some years ago, Bonnie, the daughter of a relative, died at an early age of cancer. Afterward, her mother asked Bonnie to send her a sign that she was okay. At that moment she looked up at the sky and saw a cloud in the shape of an angel. This bereaved mother's wish had been granted, and her spirit comforted.

When my dying mother was lying in bed in the living room of our family home, she would occasionally stare up into the right corner of the room. What did she see? Once, while laughing, she said it was her sister Joan, a funny storyteller who had died a few years earlier. At other times, my oldest sister was convinced our mother saw angels welcoming her into heaven. This recalls the comforting petition proclaimed during the final commendation and farewell of Catholic funerals: "Saints of God, come to her aid! Hasten to meet her, angels of the Lord!" to which those gathered respond: "Receive her soul and present her to God the Most High." That final journey from this life to the next—or in biblical imagery, the ascent from earth up the stairway to heaven (Genesis 28:12, John 1:51)—is not undertaken alone, but with the angels of God.

Angelic Influence

If believers have guardian angels at their sides throughout their life from birth to death, as the *Catechism* affirms, does the angel's presence help to make one a better person? Specifically, do these heavenly beings truly assist us on our earthly pilgrimage to summon the "better angels of our nature," so to speak? This expression occurs in the final sentence of President Abraham Lincoln's first inaugural address on March 4, 1861, when a deeply divided nation was on the verge of the most devastating war in our history. After affirming "we are not enemies, but friends," Lincoln made this proclamation that has arguably gained the status of American scripture: "The mystic chords of memory, stretching . . . to every living heart and hearthstone all over this broad land, will yet swell the chorus of the Union, when again touched, as surely they will be, by the better angels of our nature." His hope was that the populace would become unified and act upon the best instincts of its noble spirit. One commentator[34] argues that Lincoln's source may well have been Shakespeare's Othello, where "better angels" refers to praiseworthy traits that coexist alongside less admirable traits, called by some our "lesser angels." Such an appeal seems no less relevant today within a country torn apart by cultural wars and political acrimony. Many are dismayed and disheartened by divisive language on such pressing issues as immigration coming from the nation's highest office. Surely this is a time for the better angels of our nature to prevail. In the words of a Pulitzer Prize winner, "There is, in fact, no struggle more important, and none nobler, than the one we wage in the service of those better angels who, however besieged, are always ready for battle."[35]

Who are these better angels if not bearers (or supporters) of those praiseworthy traits of decency and respect, empathy and self-control, harmonious living and friendship, unity and kindheartedness? Perhaps we see our better angel as the version of ourselves who would have these traits, the better "me" we want to become by embodying them. Ruled by so-called lesser angels, on the other hand, the small-minded individual descends to acts of selfishness and divisiveness, fear and vindictiveness, envy and mean-spiritedness. Angels, or simply aspirations to "angelic" behavior, can indeed guide us and help us discern the right course of action, but ultimately we must choose whether to listen.

Listening to our better, or guardian, angels may well foster bonds of affection, the restoration of trust, and a sense of hope in a climate of darkness and despair. Anyone from right, left, or center of the ideological landscape would be hard pressed to take issue with Senator Orrin Hatch's (R-Utah) appeal in his farewell address on December 12, 2018: "If ever there were a time in our history to heed the better angels of our nature, I think it's now. How can we answer Lincoln's call to our better angels?"

Listening to one's better angels is difficult, obeying them even more so. The struggle may be as intense as what Jacob experienced when, left alone, "a man wrestled with him until daybreak" yet did not prevail (Genesis 32:24–32). In this enigmatic text, the identity of the mysterious adversary is unknown, though later the prophet Hosea dramatized the combat as one with an angel (Hosea 12:4). This interpretation is not surprising, since angels often appear as humans, as we saw with the three men who came to visit Abraham (Genesis 18:1–2). Jacob's strange visitor sought to maim him—striking him on the hip socket—yet Jacob wrestled with him through the night and prevailed, though with a wounded hip. This was his dark night of the soul.

Restraining his attacker when the fight ended, Jacob bargained for a blessing: "I will not let you go, unless you bless me" (Genesis 32:26). The blessing brought to Jacob a new name, "Israel," and hence a new identity as the leader of his people. It is instructive to note that the French verb *blesser* means "to wound," the Old English *bletsian* means "to consecrate with blood," and the English word refers to a spiritual grace and power given through gesture. The blend of connotations for blessing—violence, consecration, and spiritual grace—suggests that even in sickness or unforeseen misfortune there may be some kind of hidden blessing, which may only reveal itself with the passage of time and attentiveness to the voice of the Divine within us.

In a well-known midrash (Jewish interpretation), Jacob's surprise visitor is said to be the "patron angel of Esau," from whom Jacob obtained, through trickery, both Esau's birthright and their father's blessing (Genesis 25:29–34, 27:1–29). Was Jacob's struggle through the night with his brother Esau, or with his own shadow side of deceit—or to put it differently, with his inner demon? Another possibility is that Jacob was wrestling neither with a man nor an angel but with the very person of God, for after the fracas, the "man" explained the struggle by telling Jacob, "you have striven with God and with humans, and have prevailed" (Genesis 32:28).

The explanation that Jacob faced his own deceit is that he was engaged in an internal struggle with a demon that haunted him. How often we hear that a distraught person, especially someone with a mental illness, is struggling with "inner demons." The unfortunate association is that those with behavioral health issues are dealing with the demonic, although in rare instances this may be the case. Nancy Kehoe, who has worked for many years with spirituality groups in a psychiatric day treatment program in Boston, reframes the struggle as "wrestling with our inner angels."[36] In her moving book she describes a depressed patient who fought not to give in to bitterness and anger, a woman who strove to believe in God's goodness rather evil forces. Kehoe also narrates her own own internal struggle during a summer in turmoil, when she wrestled with the God who called her to religious life. She discloses that for most of her religious life she had been "fleeing the Hound of Heaven—and myself" (p. 114). Gradually she realized that in the mirror her patients hold up to her, "I have begun to see not a barren desert but a flowering landscape" (p. 128).

For many, guardian angels are a spiritual sign of the presence of the Divine. To those who are attentive, they provide guidance at the watershed moments of life and a tangible presence during dark moments, even moments that are insignificant in the big picture of our lives. They may also be perceived as heavenly messengers to us humans to call upon the "better angels," or virtues, of our nature and thus to make a positive difference in our community and our country.

For Reflection

- What are your thoughts about guardian angels? Do you believe some spiritual being is watching over you, and if so, how do you experience their care?

- In what ways are you called upon to summon the better angels of your nature to reflect light, trust, and hope to those around you?

Chapter Seven

Angels, Churches, and the Liturgy

The county where I grew up in southern Indiana is named after the renowned scientist, inventor, and writer Benjamin Franklin. Putting his faith in a God who created the world, sustained it, and watched over creation, Franklin envisioned a world of angels whom, he believed, communicated metaphorically through nature's beauty. He is attributed with the saying: "Flowers are the alphabet of angels, whereby they write on the hills and fields mysterious truths." Each time I return to my hometown of Brookville I am struck by the natural beauty of the rolling hills and the wildflowers, which in terms of Franklin's religious imagination communicate so much about God's goodness and "mysterious truths."

Angelic Imagery and the Church

In this same county the connection with angels is manifested through church naming: St. Michael's Church in Brookville and Holy Guardian Church in Cedar Grove (sadly, this church closed in 2013). Just to the north is St. Gabriel's and to the south is St. Peter's, named after the apostle, who had a vision of an angel in his house (Acts 11:13), who was rescued twice from prison by an angel

(Acts 5:19, 12:7), and who was even once perceived to be an angel himself (Acts 12:15). One could easily imagine, then, that this part of rural Indiana is well covered by a host of angels. The names of these churches and others like them poignantly remind the believing community that heaven and earth meet in these sacred places. We encounter not only God, but also the heavenly host, God's messengers.

As a boy who attended St. Michael's School, I looked upon this powerful archangel as my hero, a type of heavenly military warrior who conquered Satan. His statue in the school hall portrays a figure holding a shield, standing victorious, his foot subduing the head of a dragon (representing Satan, see Revelation 12:7). In the parish church, high above the main altar was a dramatic painting of St. Michael as the warrior of God who fought to vanquish evil. Perhaps this altarpiece inspires confidence in those who attend liturgies there that ultimately good will win out.

We turn from small towns in Indiana to Los Angeles, California, the second largest city in the United States. With a name meaning "The Angels" in Spanish, this huge metropolis hosts a recently completed modernistic cathedral called Our Lady of the Angels, dedicated in 2002. Across the country, a multitude of churches are named after a particular angel, the angels collectively, or Mary in association with the angels. Chicago, for example, is home to St. Mary of the Angels, Queen of Angels, and Holy Angels Churches. The first two highlight the role of Mary as above that of the angels. The third, a vibrant black parish, has a stunning mural of the Nativity overseen by a sky of angels' heads and bordered by angelic scenes from the Bible; the angels and all the figures in the scenes are dark-skinned.[37] Clearly Los Angeles and other cities so named (such as in Chile, Mexico, and Panama) have not been spared a dark underside characterized by the destructive effects of drugs, gangs, and human trafficking. But perhaps the namesakes of these cities and churches can remind us to pray all the more for their protecting help for the residents.

Among the saints in Church history closely associated with angels is St. Francis of Assisi, known as the Seraphic Father. He had a vision of Our Lady and a multitude of angels in the church of the Portiuncula in the year 1216. This event is celebrated by the Franciscans on August 2, the feast of Our Lady of the Angels.

Prayers for Heavenly Help

Besides serving as namesakes for churches and cities, angels have their place in the liturgical life of the Church and the prayers of the believing community. In the remainder of the chapter we will explore the ways in which angels appear in the worship and devotional life of the Catholic Church. At the outset it is helpful to recall an ancient Christian principle: *lex orandi, lex credendi,* Latin for "the law of praying [is] the law of believing." What the faithful express through prayer and worship is a trustworthy measure for what the faithful believe. The liturgy reflects the living faith of believers. This teaching, enunciated as early as St. Prosper of Aquitaine (c. 390–c.

465), a contemporary of St. Augustine, is reaffirmed in the *Catechism* (paragraph 1124).

Four traditional prayers prominently feature angels: Angel of God, the Litany of the Saints, the *Angelus*, and the Prayer to St. Michael the Archangel. One of the first prayers many children learn by heart begins "Angel of God, my guardian dear" (see chapter 6). When I was a child, our family often prayed it together before going to bed at night. I remember pondering then a popular holy card that depicted an angel watching over two children as they cross a wooden bridge with a missing plank. This precarious scene to be taken more figuratively than literally—I don't remember crossing many wooden bridges on foot—gave me the comforting sense of being watched over.

The second prayer is the Litany of the Saints, recited at the Easter Vigil and during other special liturgies, such as ordinations. In the roll call of this litany, heavenly beings and human saints (the friends of God) are invoked to pray for the faithful. Three archangels—Saints Michael, Gabriel, and Raphael—and two groups—"All you holy angels and archangels" and "All you holy orders of blessed spirits"— are named. After each invocation, the participants respond "pray for us." Through this litany the faithful express their communion with all the saints and angels, praying together with them. During the Feast of Saints Michael, Gabriel, and Raphael, Archangels (September 29), the faithful pray to God in the presence of the angels that "our life on earth may be defended / by those who watch over us" so that "under the faithful protection of your Angels, / we may advance boldly along the way of salvation" (Mass prayers for that feast). On October 2, the feast honoring guardian angels, the faithful are reminded of their constant care.

The third prayer is the *Angelus* (Latin for "angel"), which is prayed three times daily. Traditionally, the Angelus bell of the village church would ring at 6 am, noon, and 6 pm to remind the faithful to stop and say this prayer, which begins: "The angel of the Lord declared unto Mary" and recalls the event of the Annunciation, culminating in Mary's yes to God and the Incarnation of the Word, the Son of God (see Luke 1:26–38). On Sundays and holy days the pope leads the *Angelus* in St. Peter's Square (a custom dating back to Pope St. John XXIII); it is now live-streamed for the faithful around the world. The prayer originated in the eleventh century with the monastic practice of saying three Hail Marys at compline, or night prayer. The practice of praying the *Angelus* is portrayed in the well-known painting "The Angelus" (1857–1859), by the French artist Jean-François Millet.[38] The scene depicts two potato-harvesting peasants with heads bowed in prayer—the woman with hands folded, the man with hat removed. As a child I recall pondering this picture prominently displayed above the fireplace in the living room of my grandparents' farmhouse.

We know that the angel in the *Angelus* is Gabriel. The fourth prayer in our list similarly calls on a particular archangel. In about 1884, Pope Leo XIII had a disturbing vision during Mass, in which he heard Satan boast that he could destroy the Church and take over the world within one hundred years. Immediately after Mass the pope composed the Prayer to St. Michael the Archangel (or St. Michael Prayer), calling on the archangel to protect us "against the wickedness and snares of the devil" and "cast into hell Satan and all the evil spirits" who roam the world intent on destroying souls. He urged the faithful to pray this prayer after Mass. Many parishes still do so, and many individuals also find comfort and strength in asking the intercession of the warrior Michael in times of temptation and difficulty.

Angels and the Liturgy

The sacramental life of the Church nourishes believers from birth to death. Angels play a role in several sacraments. Although not mentioned by name in the baptismal rite, the angels nonetheless are present and active, as attested by early Christian writers.[39] Tertullian remarks: "Cleansed in the water by the action of an angel, we are prepared for the Holy Spirit. Thus, an angel is set in charge of baptism." Origen comments: "At the time that the Sacrament of Faith was administered to you, there were present heavenly powers, the ministration of the angels." St. Ambrose adds: "After Baptism you began to advance [out of the font]. The angels watched, they saw you draw near, and they suddenly beheld the splendor of your state."[40]

In the healing of the lame man at the pool of Beth-zatha in John 5:2–9, several manuscripts add after these words in verse 3, "In these [five porticoes] lay many invalids—blind, lame, and paralyzed," this explanatory text: "waiting for the stirring of the water; for an angel of the Lord went down at certain seasons into the pool and stirred up the water; whoever stepped in first after the stirring of the water was made well from whatever disease that person had." While there is no explicit reference to baptism, the action of the angel stirring the water recalls the cleansing waters of the sacrament (see John 3:3–7).

Regarding the sacrament of marriage, Tertullian again ascribes a role to the angels: "How can I ever express the happiness of a marriage joined by the Church, strengthened by an offering, sealed by a blessing, announced by angels, and ratified by the Father?"[41] One of the heavenly patrons for finding a suitable partner and for a happy marriage is the archangel Raphael, who, as we have seen, was instrumental in bringing Tobias and Sarah together.

In the Eucharist, "the source and summit of the Christian life" (*Catechism*, paragraph 1324), the faithful unite themselves "with the heavenly liturgy and anticipate eternal life" (1326). Also participating in this heavenly liturgy are the angels, whose role is mentioned several times. During the Penitential Act, the faithful confess their sinfulness first and foremost to "almighty God" and then ask "blessed Mary ever-Virgin, all the Angels and Saints . . . to pray for me to the Lord our God." The angels are called upon to pray for the gathered community in preparation for the supreme act of worship.

Then in a quick transition from penitence to praise, the Gloria is sung or recited (on solemnities and on all Sundays except during Advent and Lent). This hymn begins with the festive acclamation: "Glory to God in the highest, and on earth peace to people of good will," echoing the joyful announcement made by "a multitude of the heavenly host" to shepherds who had just received the angel's astounding news of the Messiah's birth (Luke 2:8–14). Their praise is famously enshrined in Handel's oratorio *Messiah* (1741). As believers, our ultimate destiny is to join the angels in praising the triune God in whom we live and move and have our being.

Like a recurring theme in a symphony, the preface to Eucharistic Prayer II at Mass once again calls upon the whole assembly to declare with one voice God's glory "with the Angels and all the Saints" in the "Holy, Holy, Holy." Traditionally known as the *Sanctus* in the Latin Church and the *Trisagion* ("thrice holy") in the Orthodox tradition, this joyful chant echoes that of the seraphs (the highest order of angels) whose voices shook the doorposts when the Lord called the prophet Isaiah (Isaiah 6:1–4). This prayer of the angels reminds the faithful that—despite any appearances to the contrary—heaven and earth are indeed "full of [God's] glory."

When the faithful, God's priestly people through baptism, celebrate the Eucharist with the ordained priest they do so in fellowship with the angels. The ancient sectarian community at Qumran believed they enjoyed fellowship of a liturgical nature with the priestly angels.[42] The bold claim to fellowship with the angels is highlighted in a comment made to me by Fr. Bosco Musinguzi, a Navy chaplain:

"When I celebrate Mass the angels are with me." Indeed, in fellowship with the angels, the whole community praises God with one voice in the Mass.

In recent years I had the opportunity to appreciate two remarkable artistic portrayals of angels at the eucharistic altar. One is the dramatic fifteenth century painting "Adoration of the Mystic Lamb," by the Van Eyck brothers, originally installed in St. Bavo's Cathedral (Ghent, Belgium). Surrounding a serene sacrificial lamb standing on an altar are fourteen angels.[43] The other is in the Cathedral of the Madeleine in Salt Lake City, an architectural masterpiece completed in 1909. The cathedral's stained glass windows depict a total of 258 angels. Amplifying their presence at the eucharistic liturgy are several murals of larger-than-life angels in the apse high above the main altar.

In Eucharist Prayer I of the Mass, the celebrant invokes a "holy Angel" to bring the eucharistic gifts to God's "altar on high." Similarly, we read in the Book of Revelation: "And the smoke of the incense, with the prayers of the saints, rose before God from the hand of the angel" (8:4). To summarize: whether direct or indirect, the presence of angels is evident in several parts of the Mass: they offer prayers for the penitent faithful (Confiteor), glorify God (Gloria, *Sanctus*), and bear the consecrated gifts to the heavenly altar. Through the celebration of the Eucharist the faithful encounter angels, and join with them in one voice to worship God.

Since the evangelist Luke describes a host of angels praising God, it is not surprising that a multitude of hymns with angelic themes have been written for the worshipping community to sing together. At Christmas the choices range from "Hark! The Herald Angels Sing" to "Angels We Have Heard on High" to "Ye Watchers and Ye Holy Ones." The latter hymn calls upon "seraphs, cherubim, and thrones," as well as "archangels, angels' choirs," all of whom raise their voices to sing alleluia to the Lord.

Another eucharistic hymn is the well-known *Panis angelicus* ("the bread of angels"), from a canticle composed by St. Thomas Aquinas (1225–1274)—known as the Angelic Doctor for his focus on angels. "The bread of angels," the Eucharist, is said to become "bread for humankind" (adapted translation). This theme recalls the manna from heaven provided to the Israelites in the wilderness (Exodus 16:13–15), which was explained in a later tradition as "food of angels" (Wisdom 16:20). Since angels do not need material sustenance, St. Augustine explains that angels feed on the eternal Word, Christ himself.[44]

In addition to their presence at the Eucharist, angels play a prominent role at the death of human beings, as expressed in the funeral liturgy of the Catholic Church. The prayer known in Latin as *In Paradisum* ("In Paradise") is either sung or said during the final commendation and farewell as the body is brought out of the church: "May the angels lead you into paradise; may the martyrs receive you at your arrival, and lead you to the holy city Jerusalem. May choirs of angels receive you, and with

Lazarus, once (a) poor (man), may you have eternal rest." These words may bring much comfort to the bereaved, reminding them that their loved ones who lived a life of faith are led on their journey into paradise by the angels. The physical body of the deceased will be transformed, Paul tells us, into a spiritual body characterized by glory and honor (1 Corinthians 15:42–49), and so takes on the qualities of a spiritual being, not unlike that of the angels. There are many instances throughout the world in which the dying report seeing angels at their bedside helping them on their journey to the afterlife. To give an example: one of my college students recalled that when her *abuelita* (grandmother) was dying, she saw "an angel beckoning toward stairs that lead to heaven [reminiscent of Jacob's ladder]. . . . She was talking to [the angel] like we weren't even there."

Angels in the Liturgical Year

Now, let us take a look at the Church year, which guides the faithful through the main events in the life of Jesus Christ and is anchored by the feasts of Christmas and Easter. As would be expected, angels make a prominent appearance at the beginning of the liturgical calendar, namely during Advent and Christmas. On the fourth Sunday of Advent, the Gospel readings tell about the appearance of an angel to Joseph in a dream with the startling news that Mary, to whom he is betrothed, is pregnant by the Holy Spirit (Matthew 1:18–25, Year A); or about the appearance of the angel Gabriel to Mary announcing her pregnancy in unusual circumstances (Luke 1:26–38, Year B). The appearance of the angels to the shepherds (Luke 2:8–14) is read on Christmas Day.

On the First Sunday of Lent the Gospel readings describe angels ministering to Jesus after his temptation in the desert (Matthew 4:1–11, Year A; and Mark 1:12–15, Year B; Luke 4:1–13, Year C, omits this idea but does have the devil cite Psalm 91:11–12 with reference to angels). In the Easter Vigil the Resurrection accounts either mention directly the role of the angel (Matthew 28:1–10, Year A) or a young man or men who are interpreted in later tradition to be angels (Mark 16:1–8, Year B; Luke 24:1–12 [see also 24:23], Year C).

Other stories about angels occur sporadically during Ordinary Time (the period from Pentecost to Advent). For example, Raphael's role in the story of Tobit is read during the ninth week of Ordinary Time (Year I of the weekday readings), and the appearance of the three "angels" to Abraham is heard on the Sixteenth Sunday of Ordinary Time (Year C). These instances remind the faithful of how people in biblical times experienced and described God's way of communicating with them.

In prayers and rituals, in special days and seasons in the Church year, in parishes and churches, angels are celebrated. All of these commemorations and honors are powerful reminders to believers that angels do play a supporting, though still significant, role in the lives of those on their earthly pilgrimage. Profoundly reflected in the prayer of the community is the lived faith of the community. The law of praying is the law of believing.

For Reflection

- How might greater awareness of the mention of angels in prayers, the Eucharist, and other liturgies influence your spiritual life and personal prayer?

- How have the reflections in this book influenced your own thoughts and beliefs about angels and demons?

Afterword

For centuries, celestial beings, with and without wings, have interacted with humans. In the biblical tradition they provided guidance and protection, healing and instruction. They served as divine messengers of overwhelming joy and offered direction through dreams and visions.

Angels are supernatural beings who give praise and glory to God. They do not witness to themselves and are not to be worshipped (see Colossians 2:18). Rather, they are representatives of the Holy One. As we see in the metaphor of Jacob's ladder, they convey God's loving concern to the human community, and they bring our prayers to God as Raphael did for Tobit and Sarah. In the liturgy the worshipping community joins the celebrant in asking the "holy Angel" to bring the eucharistic gifts to God's altar on high.

In the New Testament and throughout history, demons, thought to be fallen angels, have made their presence as evil spirits and cosmic powers felt, to the detriment of the believing community and humanity at large. But the evil they propagate does not have the last word, for they have been overcome by the risen Christ whose grace and power is available to all who are open to receive it.

God communicates to humankind through angelic beings, as happened with Zechariah and Mary; God also speaks directly with individuals, such as Abraham, Isaac, and Jacob, as well as Job and his friends. God spoke directly to Jesus at his baptism and Transfiguration. Above all, the Holy One has spoken through the words and deeds of Jesus to those who encountered him in person or through a revelation—as was the case with Paul (Galatians 1:12). As God's messenger *par excellence*, Jesus is called the "Angel of Great Counsel" by the Church Father Justin Martyr (100–165 AD).[45]

A few final questions to ponder: Is there sufficient evidence to embrace the reality of angels and demons, or are they merely psychological projections of divine aspirations and a rejection of any personal connection with evil, respectively? As we engage the biblical narratives and other accounts of angels and demons, perhaps we do not have to suspend critical thought to believe in them.

Why are angels growing in popularity in Western culture? Is this an indication that the broader culture is once again becoming open to a biblical perspective of the Divine, spiritual beings, the nature of good and evil, and human existence? Belief in angels provides reassurance that though God is invisible to us the Holy One has not left us alone, and that though evil is evident all around us, agents of good are at work among us too. Good has triumphed over evil once and for all through Jesus Christ, and the presence and care of angels reminds us of his victory. Hopefully, as you pondered the reflections in this brief narrative, you have become more open to recognizing the presence of the Divine through the celestial beings sent your way.

Notes

1. Andrew King, "Introduction: Angels and Demons," *Critical Survey* 23, no.4 (2011): 1–8, p. 1.

2. Uwe Wolff, "The Angels' Comeback," in R. V. Reiterer, T. Nicklas, and K. Schöpflin, *Angels: The Concept of Celestial Beings—Origins, Development and Reception* (Berlin: De Gruyter, 2006), 695–714, p. 696.

3. For example, Dan Brown, *Angels & Demons* (New York: Pocket Books Penguin Edition, 2000), a fictional drama bringing scientific terrorists into conflict with Vatican cardinals.

4. Associated Press, "Poll: Nearly 8 in 10 Americans believe in angels," December 23, 2011, https://www.cbsnews.com/news/poll-nearly-8-in-10-americans-believe-in-angels/.

5. For angels see numbers 328–336; for demons/devil, see numbers 391–395, 397–398.

6. See Matthias Köckert Berlin, "Divine Messengers and Mysterious Men in the Patriarchal Narratives of the Book of Genesis," in Reiterer, *Angels*, 51–78, p. 73.

7. See Yvette Alt Miller, *Angels at the Table: A Practical Guide to Celebrating Shabbat* (London: Bloomsbury, 2011).

8. "Babylonian Talmud: Tractate Shabbath," http://www.come-and-hear.com/shabbath/shabbath_119.html.

9. See the film *Entertaining Angels: The Story of Dorothy Day* (1996).

10. Michael Morpurgo, *On Angel Wings* (Somerville, MA: Candlewick Press, 2007).

11. Irene Nowell, "The 'Work' of Archangel Raphael," in Reiterer, *Angels*, 227–238, p. 229.

12. James H. Charlesworth, ed., *The Old Testament Pseudepigrapha*, vol. 1 (Garden City, NY: Doubleday, 1983), 32.

13. "3 Incredible Archangel Raphael Prayers for Healing," https://www.ryanhart.org/archangel-raphael-prayers/.

14. For example, Romans 8:38–39. Many writers, including Thomas Aquinas, Dante, and Milton, have followed Pseudo-Dionysius's speculative classification.

15. Rainer Maria Rilke, *Duino Elegies*, First Elegy, https://www.poemhunter.com/poem/elegy-i/.

16. Charlesworth, *Pseudepigrapha*, 15.

17. Charlesworth, *Pseudepigrapha*, 16.

18. Cynthia L. Haven, *Evolution of Desire: A Life of René Girard*, (Michigan State University Press, 2018), 204–205.

19. See Robert Barron, *Letter to a Suffering Church* (Park Ridge, IL: Word on Fire, 2019). With over a million copies in print, this book certainly strikes a chord with disillusioned Catholics, including both those who have already left the Church and others struggling to remain.

20. See Luke Timothy Johnson, "The Devil is No Joke," *Commonweal* (November 26, 2011). https://www.commonwealmagazine.org/powers-principalities.

21. Matt Baglio, *The Rite: The Making of a Modern Exorcist* (New York: Penguin Random House, 2010).

22 https://www.bostonglobe.com/2021/01/13/nation/it-was-like-looking-evil-capitol-attack-through-eyes-massachusetts-delegation/.

23. Marshall Connolly, "World Under Attack," Catholic Online, October 19, 2016, https://www.catholic.org/news/hf/faith/story.php?id=71479.

24. Russell Nieli, review of James R. Atkinson, *The Mystical in Wittgenstein's Early Writings* (New York: Routledge, 2009), https://ndpr.nd.edu/news/the-mystical-in-wittgenstein-s-early-writings/.

25. Oscar Williams, ed., *A Pocket Book of Modern Verse*, rev. ed. (New York: Washington Square, 1965), 135.

26 https://cathstan.org/news/local/one-week-after-u-s-capitol-attacked-cardinal-gregory-tells-students-we-need-the-lord-to-cast-out-the-demon-of-division-in-our-nation.

27. See, for example, David C. Downing, "Tolkien vs. Lewis on Faith and Fantasy," The Official Website of C.S. Lewis, November 14, 2012. https://www.cslewis.com/tolkien-vs-lewis-on-faith-and-fantasy/. "Tolk-

ien believed that the highest calling of the Christian artist was to be a 'sub-creator,' to create plausible and self-consistent Secondary Worlds, rather than composing tales set in the Primary World in which we live."

28. From *Andrea del Sarto*, "Ah, but a man's reach should exceed his grasp, / Or what's a heaven for?"

29. Miriam Greenspan, *Healing Through the Dark Emotions* (Boulder, CO: 2004), 255–256.

30. Junno Arocho Esteves, "Guardian angels are life's traveling companions, pope says," National Catholic Reporter, October 2, 2018. https://www.ncronline.org/news/vatican/francis-chronicles/guardian-angels-are-lifes-traveling-companions-pope-says.

31. Emma Heathcote-James, *In Seeing Angels: True Contemporary Accounts of Hundreds of Angelic Experiences* (London: John Blake, 2009 [first published in 2001]).

32. Heathcote-James, *Seeing Angels*, 75, as quoted by Dominic White, "Are Angels Just a Matter of Faith?," *New Blackfriars* 86, no. 1006 (November 2005), 568–583, p 576.

33. Darrell D. Hannah, "Guardian Angels and Angelic National Patrons in Second Temple Judaism and Early Christianity," in Reiterer, *Angels*, 413–435, p. 417.

34. David Blankenhorn, "Notes on a Phrase. 'Better Angels' In Our Past," https://www.the-american-interest.com/2019/07/04/better-angels-in-our-past/. Blankenhorn is the president of Better Angels, a citizens' organization devoted to depolarization.

35. Jon Meacham, *The Soul of America: The Battle for our Better Angels* (New York: Random House, 2018), 272.

36. Nancy Kehoe, *Wrestling with Our Inner Angels* (San Francisco: Jossey-Bass, 2009).

37. See Leo J. O'Donovan, S.J., "The 'Holy Angels' mural heralds the Gospel and one Chicago church's vibrant history," *America*, December 13, 2019, https://www.americamagazine.org/arts-culture/2019/12/13/holy-angels-mural-heralds-gospel-and-one-chicago-churchs-vibrant-history. The article includes a photograph of the mural.

38. The original painting is at the Musée d'Orsay in Paris: https://www.
musee-orsay.fr/en/collections/works-in-focus/search/commentaire_
id/the-angelus-3048.html.

39. See, for example, Fr. Basil Nortz, ORC, "Ecce Panis Angelorum:
Behold the Bread of Angels," https://www.opusangelorum.org/
English/ecce_panis_angelorum.html.

40. Msgr. Charles Pope, "The Mystical Role of the Angels in Baptism,"
February 5, 2019, http://blog.adw.org/2019/02/mystical-role-angels-
baptism/.

41. Tertullian, *Ad uxorem.* 2,8,6-7: PL 1,1412-1413; cf. *FC* 13. Cited
in the *Catechism*, number 1642.

42. 1QHa XI, 21–24.

43. The painting and an explanation of its content can be found at http://
www.jan-van-eyck.com/adoration-of-the-lamb/.

44. Basil Nortz, "*Ecce Panis Angelorum*": Behold the Bread of Angels.
Opus Sanctorum Angelorum. www.opusangelorum.org/English/
ecce_panis_angelorum.html.

45. Justin interprets Isaiah 9:6 (LXX) ("Wonderful Counselor," NRSV).
See *Dialogue with Trypho*, Chapter 76. http://www.earlychristianwrit-
ings.com/text/justinmartyr-dialoguetrypho.html.

New City Press

New City Press is one of more than 20 publishing houses sponsored
by the Focolare, a movement founded by Chiara Lubich to help
bring about the realization of Jesus' prayer: "That all may be one"
(John 17:21). In view of that goal, New City Press publishes books
and resources that enrich the lives of people and help all to strive
toward the unity of the entire human family. We are a member of
the Association of Catholic Publishers.

www.newcitypress.com
202 Comforter Blvd.
Hyde Park, New York

Periodicals
Living City Magazine
www.livingcitymagazine.com

Scan to join our mailing list
for discounts and promotions
or go to www.newcitypress.com
and click on "join our email list."